ALASKA GEOGRAPHIC

Volume 19, Number 3

KODIAK

D1501070

The Alaska Geographic Society

To teach many more to better know and more wisely use our natural resources

EDITOR
Penny Rennick

PRODUCTION DIRECTOR
Kathy Doogan

STAFF WRITER
L.J. Campbell

MARKETING MANAGER
Jan Westfall

CIRCULATION/DATABASE MANAGER
Kevin Kerns

POSTMASTER: Send address changes to
ALASKA GEOGRAPHIC®
P.O. Box 93370
Anchorage, Alaska 99509-3370

COLOR SEPARATIONS BY: Graphic Chromatics

PRINTED BY: Hart Press

PRICE TO NON-MEMBERS THIS ISSUE: $18.95

ISBN: 1-56661-004-4 (paper);
1-56661-005-2 (hardback)

COVER: *From her perch on Near Island, Lorena Christie and her retriever, Jib, survey the town of Kodiak, population 7,229, linchpin in the 280-mile-long Kodiak archipelago. (Marion Stirrup)*

PREVIOUS PAGE: *Gordon Jones fishes for silver salmon alongside his Klepper kayak in Shuyak Island State Park. (Bill Sherwonit)*

FACING PAGE: *A salmon tender is anchored off Kodiak's west side waiting for seiners to deliver their catch of pink salmon. (Matt Johnson)*

BOARD OF DIRECTORS
Richard Carlson, Kathy Doogan, Penny Rennick

Robert A. Henning, *President Emeritus*

ALASKA GEOGRAPHIC® (ISSN 0361-1353) is published quarterly by The Alaska Geographic Society, 639 West International, Unit 38, Anchorage, AK 99518. Second-class postage paid at Anchorage, Alaska, and additional mailing offices. Printed in U.S.A. Copyright © 1992 by The Alaska Geographic Society. All rights reserved. Registered trademark: Alaska Geographic, ISSN 0361-1353; Key title Alaska Geographic.

THE ALASKA GEOGRAPHIC SOCIETY is a non-profit organization exploring new frontiers of knowledge across the lands of the Polar Rim, putting the geography book back in the classroom, exploring new methods of teaching and learning—sharing in the excitement of discovery in man's wonderful new world north of 51°16'.

SOCIETY MEMBERS receive *ALASKA GEOGRAPHIC*®, a quality magazine that devotes each quarterly issue to monographic in-depth coverage of a northern geographic region or resource-oriented subject.

MEMBERSHIP in The Alaska Geographic Society costs $39 per year, $49 to non-U.S. addresses. ($31.20 of the $39 is for a one-year subscription to *ALASKA GEOGRAPHIC*®.) Order from The Alaska Geographic Society, P.O. Box 93370, Anchorage, AK 99509-3370; phone (907) 562-0164, FAX (907) 562-0479.

SUBMITTING PHOTOGRAPHS: Please write for a list of upcoming topics or other specific photo needs and a copy of our editorial guidelines. We cannot be responsible for unsolicited submissions. Submissions not accompanied by sufficient postage for return by certified mail will be returned by regular mail.

CHANGE OF ADDRESS: The post office does not automatically forward *ALASKA GEOGRAPHIC*® when you move. To ensure continuous service, please notify us six weeks before moving. Send your new address, and, if possible, your membership number or a mailing label from a recent *ALASKA GEOGRAPHIC*® to: The Alaska Geographic Society, P.O. Box 93370, Anchorage, AK 99509-3370.

MAILING LISTS: We occasionally make our members' names and addresses available to carefully screened publications and companies whose products and activities may be of interest to you. If you prefer not to receive such mailings, please advise us, and include your mailing label (or your name and address if label is not available).

ABOUT THIS ISSUE: In January 1992, staff writer L.J. Campbell got her first look at the Kodiak archipelago when she visited Kodiak and Afognak islands. Despite the unpredictable weather that brought about an unscheduled stop at Port Lions, L.J. returned to the office to research and write the bulk of this issue. Archaeologist Rick Knecht wrote the account of Kodiak's early people; teacher and principal Tom Shugak contributed personal memories of growing up on Kodiak; D. Sutherland Follows brought John Gibbons, a Kodiak cowboy, to the attention of readers; writer Irving Warner contributed "Janet Axell, Setnetter"; and *Kodiak Daily Mirror* reporter Andy Hall gave his account of Shuyak Island.

We are grateful to Kodiak residents who have shared material and reviewed the manuscript: Hank Pennington of the Fishery Industrial Technology Center; Jay Bellinger, Vic Barnes, Paul Taylor and staff of Kodiak National Wildlife Refuge; Clara Holland of Alaska State Parks; Pete Probasco of Alaska Department of Fish and Game; and Pat Carlson and others at the Kodiak Island Borough. We thank Afognak Native Corp. and their manager, Jim Carmichael, for sponsoring our writer's trip to Afognak Island. And we are grateful to Tim and Ginger Ward for providing shelter and food at Port Lions.

We appreciate the assistance of Richard Merrick with the National Marine Fisheries Service in Seattle; G. Vernon Byrd, Ed Bailey and staff of the Alaska Maritime National Wildlife Refuge; Mitch Henning with Alaska Division of Mines; Debbie Clausen with Alaska Department of Fish and Game; and Marilyn Maxwell with Koncor Forest Products. Above all this issue could not have been done without the research and review of Marian Johnson and the staff of the Kodiak Historical Society and Baranov Museum.

We also thank Marge Thera for arranging L.J.'s visit to Kodiak, and to MarkAir, which flew her to the island.

The Library of Congress has cataloged this serial publication as follows:

Alaska Geographic. v.1-
[Anchorage, Alaska Geographic Society] 1972-
v. ill. (part col.). 23 x 31 cm.
Quarterly
Official publication of The Alaska Geographic Society.
Key title: Alaska geographic, ISSN 0361-1353.

1. Alaska—Description and travel—1959-
—Periodicals. I. Alaska Geographic Society.

F901.A266   917.98'04'505   72-92087

Library of Congress 75[79112] MARC-S

Contents

Kodiak, Emerald Jewel

Trees, rocks and fishing boats poked from slate blue seas as the floatplane buzzed overhead. The plane, headed for Kodiak's harbor, was returning late in the day from Native logging operations on Afognak Island. Gathering clouds made February's early dusk even earlier. The pilot rapidly found himself flying into fog, then rain, and as landmarks disappeared, he turned the plane around.

Earlier the land had appeared in bold

A hiker surveys a portion of the interior of Kodiak Island inland from Kalsin Bay. By 1 to 2 million years ago, the Kodiak Island group resembled its present shape. During the height of the Pleistocene, more than 10,000 years ago, glaciation reached its maximum advance and most of the islands were smothered in ice. A small area of southwestern Kodiak Island, known as a refugium, likely remained ice free. As the glaciers retreated, they left U-shaped valleys and embayed shorelines. Beneath the surface, where molten rock intruded older rock, developed lode deposits of gold, silver, copper, lead, tungsten, zinc and perhaps chromium. Placer gold mingled with sand and gravel on exposed beaches. (George Wuerthner)

relief from the water, thick stands of spruce on this northern edge of Kodiak Island covering the ground with dark green spikes, the ocean breaking white on black sand beaches, rocks and islets. But now clouds, gathering thickly and quickly, muted everything. Nothing showed in the distance except gray. The pilot conversed with a crackling voice on the plane's two-way radio while scanning the horizon for a place to set down ahead of the weather and approaching dark. He passed over one after another landing spot, too icy, too foggy. Finally, a break in the sky appeared over Port Lions, a Native village northwest of Kodiak town. The plane circled, then landed in a choppy flume of water. The plane's two passengers walked up the hill into the village where a family gave them dinner and a place to sleep. The pilot would stay with his plane. He kept a sleeping bag stashed behind the seats for times like this.

Unexpected delays because of weather can happen anytime when traveling in Alaska's Bush, and few places is this more likely to happen than in the Kodiak archipelago. Stretching along the western edge of the

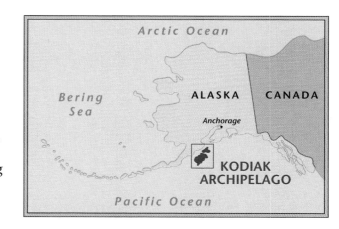

Gulf of Alaska and into the North Pacific, this collection of islands spans about 280 miles. It reaches from the Barren Islands off the Kenai Peninsula to Chirikof Island and the Semidi Islands, which were annexed in 1989 by the Kodiak Island Borough, along with an unpopulated edge of the Alaska Peninsula. With 16 major islands and dozens of smaller ones, Kodiak and its neighbors are southerly foothills, a submerged extension of the Kenai Mountains on Alaska's mainland.

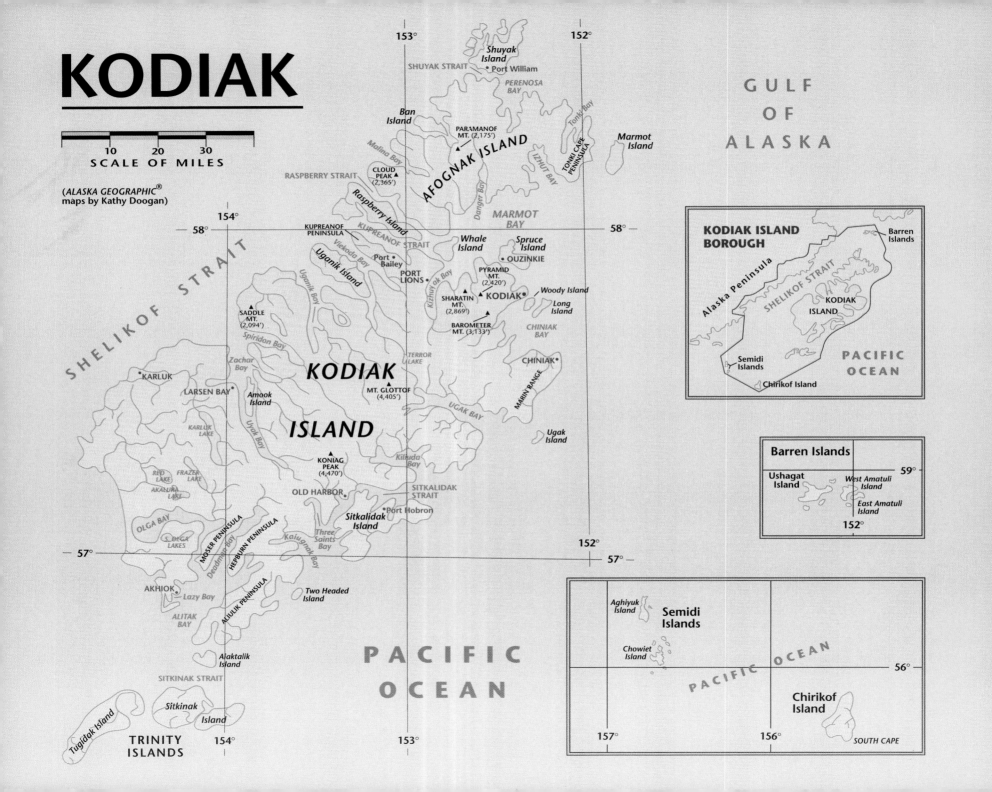

KODIAK

SCALE OF MILES

10 20 30

(*ALASKA GEOGRAPHIC*®)
maps by Kathy Doogan)

153°
152°

Shuyak Island
• Port William
SHUYAK STRAIT
PERENOSA BAY

Ban Island
Malina Bay
PARAMANOF MT. (2,175')▲
AFOGNAK ISLAND
Tonki Bay
TONKI CAPE PENINSULA
Izhut Bay
Marmot Island

GULF OF ALASKA

RASPBERRY STRAIT
CLOUD PEAK ▲ (2,365')
Danger Bay
MARMOT BAY

154°
58°
58°

Raspberry Island
KUPREANOF PENINSULA
KUPREANOF STRAIT
Viekoda Bay
Uganik Island
Whale Island
Spruce Island
• OUZINKIE

Uganik Bay
Port • Bailey
PORT LIONS •
Kizhuyak Bay
PYRAMID MT. (2,420')▲
SHARATIN MT. ▲ (2,869')
• KODIAK
• Woody Island
Long Island

SADDLE MT. ▲ (2,094')
Spiridon Bay
BAROMETER MT. (3,133')▲
CHINIAK BAY

Zachar Bay
TERROR LAKE
CHINIAK •

• KARLUK
KODIAK
Amook Island
MT. GLOTTOF ▲ (4,405')
MARIN RANGE

LARSEN BAY •
ISLAND

KARLUK LAKE
Uyak Bay
UGAK BAY
Ugak Island

RED LAKE
FRAZER LAKE
KONIAG PEAK ▲ (4,470')
Kiluda Bay

AKALURA LAKE
OLD HARBOR •
SITKALIDAK STRAIT

OLGA BAY
• Port Hobron
Three Saints Bay
Sitkalidak Island

S. OLGA LAKES
MOSER PENINSULA
HEPBURN PENINSULA
Kaluqmik Bay

57°
57°

AKHIOK •
Lazy Bay
ALIULIK PENINSULA
Two Headed Island

ALITAK BAY
DEADMAN BAY

Aiaktalik Island

SITKINAK STRAIT

Tugidak Island
Sitkinak
Island

TRINITY ISLANDS

154°
153°

PACIFIC OCEAN

KODIAK ISLAND BOROUGH

Barren Islands
Alaska Peninsula
SHELIKOF STRAIT
KODIAK
• ISLAND
Semidi Islands
PACIFIC OCEAN
Chirikof Island

Barren Islands

Ushagat Island
West Amatuli Island
East Amatuli Island
59°
152°

Aghiyuk Island
Semidi Islands
Chowiet Island
PACIFIC OCEAN
56°

Chirikof Island
SOUTH CAPE

157°
156°

SHELIKOF STRAIT

The Kodiak Island group is anchored by Kodiak Island, largest in Alaska and second to Hawaii as the largest island in the United States. Kodiak's 3,620 square miles are pinched into snow-covered peaks topping 4,300 feet, a spiny backdrop for a coastline that seems to endlessly bend and jag. Capes, peninsulas, bays and steep-sided fiords give the island more than 1,274 miles of zigzagging coast. Some fingers of water, like Uyak Bay off Shelikof Strait on the west and Deadman Bay off Alitak Bay on the south, reach inland so far as if to prick the island in two. Some of the first Russians to visit Kodiak in the late 1700s determined that no place on the island was more than 15 miles from ocean, and today that is still the official line. The exception to Kodiak's rugged coast occurs at the island's southwestern corner, where the shoreline smooths with spits and sandbars. Here broad alluvial valleys, lowlands, shallow lagoons, lakes and meandering rivers occur in marked contrast to the island's mountainous interior, which drains in steep, short streams flowing to deeply indented bays. Through this southwestern corner flow the island's two longest rivers, the Ayakulik and Karluk, which are each only about 30 miles. Here also is found Karluk Lake, the island's biggest and nursery for one of the largest sockeye salmon populations in the world.

The region's maritime climate, with moderate temperatures and plenty of moisture, turns Kodiak into a lush, green paradise in summer, so much so that travel brochures call it Alaska's "Emerald Isle." The Spanish during a stopover in 1788 apparently saw the island blanketed with the blooms of salmonberries, raspberries, beach

ABOVE: *Tidepoolers search for sea urchins, sea stars, sea cucumbers, sponges, chitons, limpets, nudibranchs and octopi among the rocks of Womens Bay on Kodiak Island. (David Menke)*

RIGHT: *Emperor geese forage among seaweed along Chiniak Bay. Emperors breed in coastal marshes and tundra of western Alaska, and winter along seashores in the Aleutians, Alaska Peninsula and Kodiak. (David Menke)*

strawberries, devil's club and mountain ash, and called it "Florida Blanca." On sunny, clear days, winter or summer, Kodiak's scenery is breathtaking. Cloudy days, however, are most typical since skies are completely overcast more than half the time, yet even then the place exudes dramatic beauty. Of course a prolonged period of soggy skies — Kodiak averages 74 inches of rain a year with some spots getting as much as 200 inches — can prompt even the diehard island fan to escape "the rock." The weather can make for dicey travel, particularly since everyone and everything

Hunters Tony Ledbetter and Jim Simmen warm themselves during an outing on Afognak Island. While most of Afognak and parts of Shuyak are forested, the tree line for spruce has been creeping southwest on Kodiak Island at about a mile per century. (Jim Simmen)

comes in and out by plane or boat. Mail planes and local air taxis may wait days for flying weather, particularly in winter, the wettest season.

Temperatures here are moderate, averaging 50 to 60 degrees in summer and the low 20s in winter. Snowfall averages 6 feet a year in some places, enough for occasional sledding and telemark skiing; but none of it sticks around long in the lowlands. Although ice coats a few of the more shallow bays in winter, floatplane pilots do not even bother to equip their planes with skis. This frustrates the ice and alpine climbing enthusiasts in Kodiak who would like to tackle the island's backcountry

peaks but do not have the week or so needed to bushwack in by foot.

The air and sea currents that bring these moderate temperatures can also whip up some nasty winds. Area fishermen are well aware of the hazards, particularly in winter when gales douse boat decks and rigging with freezing spray. Crews caught in this predicament have to hammer on the ice with axes and bats to keep their vessels from becoming top-heavy catastrophes.

Kodiak means different things to different folks. To big game hunters and photographers, it means Kodiak bears, reputed to be the world's biggest, fiercest land predators. To the U.S. Coast Guard, Kodiak is its biggest base and launching point for some of the most dangerous rescue missions going into the North Pacific and Bering Sea. Sport and commercial fishermen know Kodiak for its salmon runs and bustling port.

It is a region rich with fish. Kodiak, Afognak, Shuyak and Raspberry islands are crisscrossed by some of the most fertile salmon streams in the world. The Karluk River on Kodiak became famous during the late 1800s when half a dozen salmon canneries at the river's mouth made it the busiest fishing area in the territory. The earliest people of Kodiak and its neighboring islands were mariners, living on land closest to water where they fished and hunted mostly sea animals.

The sea churning through the archipelago teems with life. In addition to the five species of salmon, halibut are abundant, herring are found in almost all the bays, and populations of Tanner crab and Dungeness crab are sufficient to support commercial

harvest. Shrimp, scallops, urchins for their roe, and even a small amount of coral for jewelry have been taken by area fishermen. King crab, so plentiful that its harvest in 1968 boosted Kodiak to the top port in the nation in dollar value, provided steady fishing until the late 1970s when stocks crashed. In the past decade, groundfish such as pollock, Pacific cod and sablefish have become important commercial commodities.

The archipelago, with its many islands offering rocky cliffs, marshy lowlands, forests and thickets, attracts more than 215 species of birds. The Barren and Semidi islands and Tugidak Island shelter large breeding populations of seabirds, including forked-tailed storm-petrels, puffins, murres and fulmars. At least 200 pairs of bald eagles nest on Kodiak, Uganik, Ban and Afognak islands. An estimated 1.5 million seabirds winter on just the islands closest to Kodiak, along with some 150,000 waterfowl. About 56 species of birds live on Kodiak Island year-round. They include black-capped chickadees, nuthatches, thrushes, magpies, ravens, pine grosbeaks, bald and golden eagles and glaucous-winged and mew gulls.

Spring migration begins in April with tundra swans and brants en route to Izembek Lagoon on the Alaska Peninsula. The most abundant migrants are ducks such as northern pintails, mallards, green-winged teals and northern shovelers; and shorebirds, such as plovers, western and least sandpipers, common snipes and wandering tattlers. Small land birds — swallows, thrushes, warblers, sparrows and the like — arrive early to mid-May. Fall migration may begin as early as July or as late as the end of October.

The first recorded observations and

ABOVE: *Bald eaglets cast a steady gaze from their nest on Tugidak Island, one of the Trinity Islands just southwest of Kodiak. While normally nesting in trees, bald eagles build nests on grassy headlands near water when trees are not available. (David Menke)*

TOP RIGHT: *One of two puffin species found along Alaska's coastline from the Chukchi Sea to Southeast, these tufted puffins gather near the top of Zaimka Island at the mouth of Womens Bay. (David Menke)*

RIGHT: *A male orange-crowned warbler feeds on an insect near Kalsin Bay. Fairly nondescript as Alaska's warblers go, the male is only slightly more yellowish overall than the female. This species usually lives in brushy woodlands and feeds from low branches. (David Menke)*

collections of birds from Kodiak and its neighbors came from naturalist Carl Merck, who was aboard a Russian ship commanded by Englishman Joseph Billings. Merck collected through winter 1789 and spring 1790, then sent his findings to Peter Simon Pallus in St. Petersburg, who produced the first scientific record of Kodiak bird life.

Observed then were geese, auk, blue petrel and black guillemot divers, and Natives using ducks for food and clothing and puffin bills for ornamentation. A later Russian visitor, Capt. Urey Lisiansky, wrote in 1805 that he saw a tame eagle fly into a Native home and settle itself by the fireside where it fell asleep. The eagle, he was told, was so sagacious that it would recognize at sea the bidarkas of its master and follow them home from fishing. The islanders, he observed, tamed eagles for their feathers to use for arrows.

So many fossils have been found along the beach below Cliff Point at the south entrance to Womens Bay that residents have dubbed the area Fossil Beach. (Roz Goodman)

More than 20 species of marine mammals live in the coastal waters of Kodiak The most abundant are sea otters, harbor seals, Dall and harbor porpoises and Steller sea lions.

Sea otters, almost hunted to extinction by the Russians and then the Americans from the mid-1700s through 1911 when commercial hunting was banned, are rebounding. In 1992, they were estimated to number about 13,000 and found in most bays around Afognak and Kodiak islands. Natives are allowed to harvest sea otters and use their furs to make handcrafts for sale. Because sea otters feed on such shellfish as crab and sea urchins, their expanding population may run afoul in the near future of people trying to harvest the same species.

Several species of whales have been spotted in Kodiak waters. Humpback, fin and gray whales migrate through on their way to and from the Bering and Chukchi seas each spring and fall. Brad Hanson, a National Marine Fisheries Service biologist, recalls seeing a spectacular gathering of about 125 killer whales, a superpod aggregation that stretched across the horizon east of Marmot Island in 1987. Beaked whales and minke whales also have been spotted, but these sightings are less common.

Harbor seals haul out on sandy beaches and sand bars of the archipelago to breed and have pups. At one time, the Kodiak Island group had the world's largest known population of harbor seals.

The island group also had the world's largest Stellar sea lion rookery, until recent years brought a decrease in sea lion populations. Steller sea lions have declined at an alarming rate throughout their range from Kenai to Kiska Island in the Aleutians, dropping 63 percent rangewide since 1971. Several rookeries and haul-outs still exist in the Kodiak island group. During the 1970s and 1980s, Marmot Island was the largest Steller sea lion rookery in the world until population declines here dropped numbers below that of Forester Island, off the coast of Prince of Wales Island in southeastern Alaska.

No one knows why sea lion numbers are dropping. Disease, competition with fishermen for pollock, a mainstay in the sea lion diet, and tangles in fishing nets are all thought to play a part. Juvenile sea lions in particular are having a tough time surviving. In December 1990, the Steller sea lion was listed as threatened by the Endangered Species Act, and three-mile no-entry zones were set up around rookeries. In 1991 "no trawl" zones were established around the rookeries to keep fishing boats at least 10 miles away. Fishermen and sea lions are far from close buddies — sea lions have raided fishing nets and fishermen have been known to shoot them because of it. Fishermen have also shot sea lions and other marine mammals for bait. In general these excesses have been curbed, and fishermen work with the scientists to determine what might be causing the crash of sea lion and harbor seal populations. The "no trawl" restrictions cut into commercial fishing territory, but the situation could be worse. Should sea lion populations continue to decline and the animal's status be elevated to "endangered," fishing could be closed down entirely.

In at least one place, however, the sea lions seem to be holding their own. That is in downtown Kodiak at the boat harbor, where they are sometimes fed by fishermen, a practice banned by city ordinance and federal law. Sea lions haul out on the docks and sometimes climb aboard unoccupied fishing boats looking for food. Their hulking presence has led to more than a few incidents of almost legendary status. Take the time, for instance, when the sea lion jumped out of the water and bit a fisherman on his rump.

Kodiak Island is the most populated of the island group, by far. It is home to most of the borough's 15,535 people, most living in Kodiak town and others scattered about the island's fringe in small Native villages and cannery camps. Kodiak is also populated by some 3,000 brown bears, one of the densest populations of wild bears in the world, and they live wherever they want.

These Kodiak bears have brought the island worldwide fame. Wealthy hunters fly here to hunt trophy bears, spending $10,000 or better for a guided trip into the island's dense brush. Wildlife lovers and photographers also thrill at the sight of these bruins. In 1992, more than 260 people applied for 90 spaces at a new U.S. Fish and

Wildlife Service bear viewing platform on the south bank of Karluk Lake, where the bears congregate to feed on salmon.

So treasured a national resource is the Kodiak bear that two-thirds of Kodiak Island, plus Ban and Uganik islands and part of Afognak Island, are set aside as Kodiak National Wildlife Refuge, expressly for the purpose of protecting bears and their habitat. Not all islanders are happy about this, and blame the "Bear Farm" when the bears cause problems in town and the villages. In 1992, the question of protecting the bears took a new twist. Native

BELOW: *Eunice Neseth, born on Afognak in 1907 and raised on the island, gathers beach rye for use in her Aleut basket-weaving class. The daughter of a Swedish storeman, Eunice retired from teaching, started the museum at Kodiak and taught basket-weaving for a number of years. (Roz Goodman)*

RIGHT: *This trail leads to Mulcahy View public use cabin in Shuyak Island State Park. (Bill Sherwonit)*

corporations launched a media blitz to gain support for federal buy-back of Native lands within the refuge. One newspaper and magazine after another —*Time, Newsweek, Esquire, The Los Angeles Times, The London Times* — published articles about Native corporations' plans to build tourist resorts on refuge inholdings and to clearcut all Native lands on nearby Afognak Island, unless their property is bought by the government.

Afognak Island, the second largest island in the group, has thick forests dominated by Sitka spruce. During the last ice age, which

ended 10,000 to 15,000 years ago, glaciers extended over most of the Kodiak archipelago, sculpting the mountainous uplands and scouring out valleys. Today, a few receding glaciers remain at higher elevations on Kodiak Island. In general, the glaciers plowed away any existing tree

Near Island, Woody Island and Long Island appear in this overview of downtown Kodiak. Founded by the Russians two centuries ago, the community's 7,229 residents rely on fishing, fish processing, fisheries research, tourism, logging, services and the U.S. Coast Guard to support its economy. (Steve McCutcheon)

growth in what became the Kodiak Island group. The spruce on Afognak Island and the northeastern edge of Kodiak Island became established within the last 400 to 600 years, and the forest front is migrating at a rate of about a mile each 100 years. The species periodically leapfrogs perhaps even more rapidly, according to John Alden, research forester at the Institute of Northern Forestry in Fairbanks.

The southwestern corner of Kodiak Island apparently escaped glaciation. This area, known as the Kodiak refugium, has the land form and plant life of the high Arctic. For instance, a heather typical of the Arctic is

found here near sea level. Some plants and insects found here are thought to appear nowhere else on Kodiak.

Otherwise, thickets of alder, salmonberry and blueberry, and shrubs and grasses cover the island. Alder grows profusely from near salt water to elevations of more than 2,000 feet. Willows are more common in moist areas on the southern part of the island. Cottonwood groves dot lakeshores and river bottoms, while bluejoint grass and fireweed grow into thick meadows. Birch trees are found only in lower elevations. Other common lowland plants are highbush cranberry, horsetail, cow parsnip, seacoast angelica and sedges. Along the shores grow beach rye used in basketry. Alpine areas nurture crowberry, bearberry, alpine azalea, cranberry, mosses, lichens and sedges.

The island serves up quite a smorgasbord for those who know how to use and harvest wild edible plants. During a course on the subject in spring 1992, students concocted a potluck dinner of such dishes as fiddlehead fritters, violet salads, beach greens, nettle casseroles and pond lily root sauce, with devil's club root tea, dandelion wine and berry pies for dessert.

Each summer, gardeners on Kodiak take advantage of seaweed, a natural fertilizer washed ashore by the ocean. They use pitchforks, shovels and buckets to collect the piles of "beach peat," a mixture rich with fish bones, shells and kelp, to spread on their gardens and to mix into compost piles. Using seaweed as a soil conditioner on Kodiak goes back to gardens kept by the Natives for the Russians.

Originally, the islands had only a few types of animals, mainly bears, red foxes, land otters, short-tailed weasels, little brown bats and small rodents like the tundra vole. The Russians brought the first cattle to the islands in 1794 and horses sometime later. With dubious success, cattle ranching continues today, many of the animals ranging free along Chiniak Bay. At various times this century, the Alaska Game Commission attempted to expand the region's limited indigenous animal population with a variety of other animals. Some introductions took, others did not. Roosevelt elk, beaver, Sitka black-tailed deer, snowshoe hare, mountain goat, muskrat, caribou and red squirrel survived and spread. Dall sheep, moose and mink introductions failed.

The Sitka deer introduction may be the most successful. The deer are found throughout Kodiak Island, on most of small, nearby islands and have reached all the way to Sitkinak Island on the south and Afognak, Shuyak and Marmot islands to the north. The first 14 deer were released on Long Island in 1924 with another nine let loose on Kodiak in 1934. The animals suffered during harsh winters in the late 1960s, but their population exploded during the following two decades. The animals swim island to island, and sometimes their attempts fail. In two separate incidents, large numbers of deer have been found dead on the beaches of Tugidak Island, where they apparently drowned in the currents during a crossing from Kodiak or Sitkinak islands.

Hunting these deer in recent years has become a popular pastime as well as being something of an economic boomlet for Kodiak. Between 4,000 and 5,000 hunters were in the field during the 1991 season, August through December, and more than

half were people from off the island.

The elk on Afognak and neighboring Raspberry are the continent's northernmost herds. Roosevelt elk were brought to Litnik (Afognak) Bay on Afognak Island in spring 1929. By 1958, five major herds lived in the southwest corner of Afognak and on neighboring Raspberry Island. A series of population peaks and dives due to harsh winters in the intervening years has brought elk populations to about 1,000 animals. Occasionally mass die-offs occur, like in 1986 when 40 some elk were found dead in a pile on an Afognak Island beach. It was the middle of hunting season. They had apparently run off a cliff about 500 feet above. Elk occasionally are spotted on Kodiak, apparently having swum from Afognak, but Kodiak Island has no established herd.

Reindeer appeared on Kodiak in 1924 when 32 animals were brought to the southern end of the island for herding. In the 1930s, they escaped from their handlers and were allowed to remain free. At that time, the herd was estimated at about 1,500 animals. For the past decade, reindeer numbers have stabilized at 200 to 300, and

they are found on a small portion of southwestern Kodiak Island.

Southwestern Alaska's only mountain goats are found on Kodiak Island. The

Waves lap the shore of Kalsin Bay beneath snowy summits of the Marin Range on Kodiak Island. (Don Pitcher)

current population of about 500 goats found throughout the island sprung from 18 goats introduced at Hidden Basin in 1952.

The people who live on these islands reside in a land plentiful with wild game, fish and berries, where stunning scenery wraps in every direction. The island's abundant natural resources supported thousands of Native Koniags in early times, making it one of the most densely populated parts of Alaska.

The region's resources have always been its drawing card, first to the Russian fur traders and later to American salmon processors. Its location brought the U.S. military during World War II, which transformed the quiet fishing village of Kodiak into bustling Army and Navy bases. Today, its resource base and proximity to some of the world's richest fishing grounds continue to attract people. "The things you see here," says Bud Cassidy, a former fisherman who now works as the borough lands resource management officer. "Killer whales swimming across Shelikof Strait, thousands of salmon leaping in the air, bears swimming across the bay. That's why you stay."

The place is growing; since 1980, the Kodiak Island Borough has experienced a steady 4 percent population growth annually, not including seasonal workers who come to town to crew in the canneries or on boats. The ethnic diversity includes Filipinos, who once held most of the low-paying cannery jobs but now are running taxi services and other small business, and Hispanics, who have moved into the lower paying processing jobs. The makeup of the fisheries, in the meantime, has changed from seasonal salmon, crab and shrimp harvesting and processing to year-round work with groundfish, such as pollock and Pacific cod.

The borough and city are undertaking a variety of new projects. A $26 million breakwater is going in to accommodate boats up to 100 feet; an expansion of the sewer and water treatment system is in the works; a new floatplane harbor is going in on the east side of Near Island along with a road around the island and areas slated for business development. A bridge to Near Island built in 1986 once went nowhere, now it goes somewhere, quips borough mayor Jerome Selby.

Services and businesses likewise have expanded. Most of the statewide financial institutions operate branches here, three car dealership sell new and used vehicles, and there are 250 hotel rooms, several bed and breakfasts, numerous restaurants, and even a guest ranch with beachfront horseback riding on the edge of town. Fast food franchises have sprung up. In 1986, Safeway Inc. opened the town's first 24-hour grocery, a big event that drew a parking lot full of people who held tailgate picnics and barbecues in anticipation of the midnight grand opening. Meantime, O. Kraft & Son, the homegrown grocery and general store that has operated in Kodiak since 1903, has regrouped. Kraft bought out another locally owned grocery and acquired ownership of village stores in Port Lions and Larsen Bay. Both groceries do a substantial business supplying fishing fleets, and locals sometimes find the shelves nearly bare after boats unexpectedly pull into port.

Picturesque downtown Kodiak offers hours of diversion. From its bustling waterfront with St. Paul harbor and the state ferry dock, the main shopping district stretches west, filling a flat pocket at the foot of Pillar Mountain. The town climbs steeply to the north, with residential areas and businesses spilling northeast along the main drags to Spruce Cape and Mill Bay. The bright blue onion-shaped domes of the Holy Resurrection Orthodox Church are a distinct downtown landmark, and the mountainsides above town are layered with wooden homes. In 1991, heavy rains brought on a mudslide that wiped out a number of them.

Visitors can check in at a visitor's center in the Chamber of Commerce building on Marine Way next to the ferry dock for an update on local happenings. The big ship that looks like it is plowing into the road is supposed to be here, by the way. It is the *Star of Kodiak*, an old liberty ship brought in as a cannery after the 1964 earthquake. The harbormaster's office nearby is the pulse of the region, keeping tabs on the 770 boats that homeport here plus hundreds of other vessels coming in and out. The Fisherman's Memorial outside the office is a tribute to the men and women lost at sea. Each year, a ceremony is held during which bells toll as names of the dead are read aloud. Flowers then are thrown into the harbor with a priest's blessing.

The Baranov Museum in the Erskine House, a log structure originally used as a fur warehouse by Alexander Baranov, manager of the Russian American Co., is home of the Kodiak Historical Society. The society's collection gives a good perspective on the region's prehistory, and Russian and American periods, as well as fine arts. Curators have compiled a dozen or so photo albums on various topics, which are available to visitors. A small collection of Russian Orthodox artifacts can be seen at the Veniaminov Museum, located in St. Herman's Orthodox Theological Seminary several blocks up the hill from the Baranov Museum. The Kodiak Area Native Association has a large collection of precontact and postcontact Koniag pieces, some of which are on display at KANA offices downtown. Eventually this collection will be transferred to a Native cultural museum to be built on Near Island.

Kodiak is large enough to support a number of stores, and those clustered downtown including bookstores, cafes, gift shops and drugstores. Kodiak's only movie theater, the Orpheum, is downtown. A showplace gone seedy, its once-plush, red-and-black sculptured carpet is threadbare in places, with spots of spilled soda pop and squashed Milk Duds. Sheets of silver tinsel hang on each side of the single-screen auditorium in the middle of big bare walls. But $6 for a front row balcony seat buys quite the experience on a Friday night, the theater filled to capacity with kids hooting at each other and sometimes watching the feature presentation, which on this night was "Beauty and the Beast."

Another side to Kodiak's culture can be found up the road, at the new performing arts center in the high school. This $10.5 million facility features a 500-seat main house and two smaller pods, each seating 125 people, that can be hydraulically revolved to face the main stage. A production's success is judged these days on whether it was a one-pod or two-pod

John Garber (blue sweater) washes a sluice at his small beach placer operation on Tugidak Island, while John Preston looks on. Midge Garber (in red hat) chats with Joe Sautner of the state's Department of Environmental Conservation. Tugidak Island was designated a Critical Habitat Area in 1988 and is closed to new mineral entry. (M.W. Henning, Alaska Division of Mines)

Richard Merrick puts a satellite-linked radio transmitter on the back of a Steller sea lion. The transmitter collects data on the depth the animal dives, and when the sea lion surfaces, the transmitter sends a signal to the satellite. If the satellite can pick up enough data on when the animal surfaces, scientists will be able to determine where the animal goes to feed. (Bob Hallinen, Anchorage Daily News)

show, says Gerald Wilson, executive director of the Kodiak Arts Council. The arts council manages the center, booking a performing arts series, a summer fine arts program for children, and several locally produced plays and concerts each year. Kodiak has several performing groups including a traditional chamber orchestra and choir, Russian dancers, Aleut dancers, a group of balalaika (Russian folk instrument) players.

Rezanof Drive goes northeast and southwest out of downtown. Kodiak has less than 100 miles of road, and Rezanof is the central artery. In 1992, this state-owned road was a series of potholes for which the city was trying to get maintenance money. From downtown, Rezanof Drive West leads to the airport, the Kodiak National Wildlife Refuge headquarters, the U.S. Coast Guard base and Buskin River State Recreation Site. This road continues along the shoreline of Chiniak Bay to Cape Chiniak, about 42 miles of dips and curves around Womens Bay, Middle Bay and Kalsin Bay, through majestic stands of Sitka spruce and nobby hills of scrub alders. About 150 people live at the end of the Chiniak road, where a school and post office are located along with an abandoned World War II airstrip. Off this road are gravel turnoffs going to Anton Larsen Bay, Saltery Cove and Pasagshak Bay. Take Rezanof Drive northeast from town to the outlying business and residential district. This road leads past Fort Abercrombie State Park and the amphitheater where the state's oldest running play, "Cry of the Wild Ram," is held each August. The road eventually ends about 12 miles later at Monashka Bay. The Point Otmeloi hiking trail starts here.

Those who live here fill their year with work and play, everything from fly-fishing to clam digging to bird watching to kayaking. In the spring, there is the Crab Festival, a weekend celebration, that includes the Chad Ogden Memorial Run, 42 miles from Chiniak to town, and the Pillar Classic, a 15-kilometer mountain race. "It's hard," says Jim Bruskotter, manager of O. Kraft's who runs in the Pillar Classic, up the road through snow then basically cross-country down the mountain's back side. "The next day your upper thighs are in massive pain." Pillar Mountain is also the site each March of the Pillar Mountain Golf Classic, a one-hole par-70 tournament where caddies are as likely to carry chain saws as putting irons.

So what is living in Kodiak like? Ask a room full of third graders at East Elementary and they will talk nonstop. "It rains a lot, but it's really nice," chirps a girl named LeeAnn, who says she likes to hike up Pillar Mountain near town. Robyn adds, "It's green green in the summer." Kaitlyn mentions the bears, including one that came into the Pizza Hut parking lot last winter. After that, they did not walk anywhere without a friend, she said. One girl told about fishing with her family when a bear on shore charged their skiff. Her classmate had the wildest story of all: She was playing in the yard with her cousin and an eagle swooped down and pecked her cousin's neck and made it bleed.

Everyone, of course, has their own version of why they like Kodiak. Turn on a locally produced tape called "Life on the Island" for a few verses of the lament "King Crab, Where Did You Go," or "Rusty Tuste," a song about the ferry, or "Watching the Wildlife in Kodiak AK" that speaks to the wildlife crawling out of the bars.

And then there is the view of those who know Kodiak from the water in. Stacy Studebaker, an avid kayaker, is one of those. "Kodiak is like nowhere else. Everywhere you go is just magnificent," she says. "You're traveling a shoreline you've never seen before, looking for a campsite, a nice beach with steep gravel for landing, a stream with water. You find it, pull up and look above the tide line in the grass and find barabara holes, where someone lived thousands of years ago. You reach out your hand during lunch on a sunny beach and there's a labret or a stone scraper that a human hand made long ago. Its a magic place."

Kodiak Island and Its Neighbors

(ALASKA GEOGRAPHIC®
maps by Kathy Doogan)

Outlined areas refer to detailed maps on the following pages.

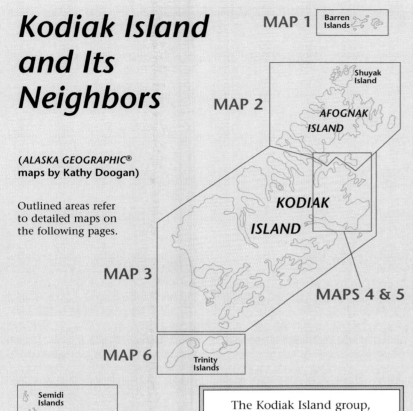

Note: *Land areas come from 1992 estimates from the Kodiak Island Borough's computerized digitized mapping system, and the U.S. Bureau of Land Management, except for Chirikof Island whose land area is from the U.S. Geological Survey. All Steller sea lion rookeries are protected by a three-mile no-entry zone and a 10-mile no-trawl zone because Steller sea lions are listed as threatened under the Endangered Species Act.*

The Kodiak Island group, located in the western Gulf of Alaska on the edge of the continental shelf, includes more than 100 islands ranging in size from Alaska's largest, Kodiak, to unnamed islands of bare rock. In 1989, the Kodiak Island Borough extended its boundaries to include Chirikof and the Semidi islands to the south, and a portion of the Alaska Peninsula to the west.

On the following pages we take a closer look at some of Kodiak's island neighbors.

BARREN ISLANDS (map 1):
Seven named islands 18 miles south of the Kenai Peninsula form the northern boundary of the Kodiak Island Borough. The three largest islands are included in the Alaska Maritime National Wildlife Refuge, Gulf of Alaska Unit. The Barrens support about 500,000 birds representing 14 species, including one of the largest colonies in the Gulf of Alaska. The larger islands offer long sand beaches, cliffs, mountains and lakes. The smaller islands feature steep terrain and rocky cliffs.

Ushagat: 7 square miles (4,480 acres); maximum elevation 1,935-foot Ushagat Peak. Steller sea lion haul-outs. Most heavily used of Barrens by migrant shorebirds. Breeding loons and grebes.

West Amatuli: 2.66 square miles (1,705 acres); maximum elevation 1,358 feet. 1,200 pelagic cormorants, 300 red-faced cormorants, 93,000 tufted puffins.

East Amatuli: 1.66 square miles (1,065 acres); maximum elevation 1,539-foot Puffin Peak. Fork-tailed storm-petrels, 11,000 to 28,000 black-legged kittiwakes, 88,500 common murres, 1,200 thick-billed murres. Pigeon guillemots, ancient murrelets, marbled murrelets, northern fulmars and 74,000 tufted puffins nest here.

Sugarloaf: .28 square miles (180 acres); maximum elevation 1,210 feet. Major Steller sea lion rookery; migratory stopover for northern fur seals. 30,000 seabirds including

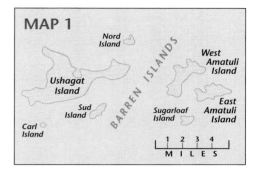

10,000 fork-tailed storm-petrels; 8,000 tufted puffins, 1,600 glaucous-winged gulls and lesser numbers of pigeon guillemots, black oystercatchers and cormorants.

Nord: .13 square miles (85 acres); maximum elevation 690 feet. Black-legged kittiwakes, 30,000 common murres. A colony of 500 parakeet auklets are near the eastern end of their range.

Sud: .47 square miles (300 acres); maximum elevation 980 feet. Harbor seals along the coast. Small Steller sea lion haul-out. About 23,000 seabirds including 1,500 rhinoceros auklets. Also fork-tailed storm-petrels, glaucous-winged gulls, tufted and horned puffins and parakeet auklets. Introduced marmots, rabbits and ground squirrels. Remnants of World War II concrete bunker high on island.

Carl: .05 square miles (30 acres); maximum elevation 75 feet; Steller sea lion haul-out. 1,000 seabirds including tufted and horned puffins and red-faced cormorants.

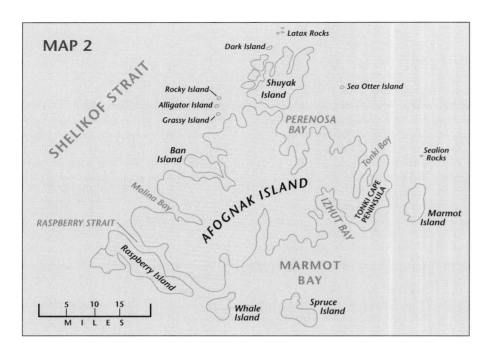

MAP 2

Latax Rocks
Dark Island
SHELIKOF STRAIT
Rocky Island
Alligator Island
Grassy Island
Shuyak Island
Sea Otter Island
PERENOSA BAY
Ban Island
Tonki Bay
Sealion Rocks
Molina Bay
AFOGNAK ISLAND
TONKI CAPE PENINSULA
Marmot Island
RASPBERRY STRAIT
IZHUT BAY
Raspberry Island
MARMOT BAY
Whale Island
Spruce Island

5 10 15
M I L E S

SHUYAK (map 2):

69.2 square miles; maximum elevation 660 feet; 11,000 acres on west and north designated Shuyak Island State Park in 1984. Remnant colony of sea otters now spread throughout the archipelago; rich concentrations of seabirds in-cluding three species of cormorants

AFOGNAK (map 2):

708.1 square miles ; maximum elevations, Red Peak (2,425 feet), Cloud Peak (2,365 feet), Afognak Mountain (2,255 feet). Roosevelt elk introduced in 1929; muskrats introduced 1925, snowshoe hares 1934, and marten and red squirrels in 1952. Other mammals include beaver, land otter, red fox, Sitka black-tailed deer and brown bears. Marbled murrelets, subject of

intense scientific scrutiny because little is known of their nesting habitats, have been known to nest on the island.

Designated Afognak Forest and Fish Culture Reserve in 1892, one of the first wildlife preserves in the nation; island transferred to Chugach National Forest in 1908. Some logging during World War II by U.S. Army. Most of island conveyed to Native ownership under Alaska Native Claims Settlement Act and Alaska National Interest Lands Conservation Act; 40,600 acres in the northwest corner added to Kodiak National Wildlife Refuge; 75,000 acres around Afognak Lake are Chugach National Forest. Logging underway by Native owners. Kodiak Regional Aquaculture Association operates Kitoi Bay hatchery.

BAN (map 2):

11 square miles (7,040 acres); maximum elevation 2,130 feet. Entire island added to Kodiak National Wildlife Refuge in 1980.

LESSER ISLANDS OF SHUYAK AND AFOGNAK (map 2):

Seals and Steller sea lions haul out on reefs and rocks near all these islands.

Grassy: .02 square miles (10 acres). Group of small islets with 200 tufted puffins, 20 glaucous-winged gulls, 10 cormorants and an undetermined number of nocturnal nesting birds.

Alligator: .03 square miles (20 acres).

Rocky: .008 square miles (5 acres).

Sea Otter: .07 square miles (45 acres). Steller sea lion haul-out; sea otters, harbor seals. Nesting teals, mallards, gadwalls, mergansers; several nocturnal seabirds, 3,000 diurnal seabirds including tufted and horned puffins, parakeet auklets, pelagic cormorants and glaucous-winged gulls. Brown bears sometimes swim to the island to feed on birds.

Dark: .31 square miles (200 acres). Teals, mallards, mergansers, red-throated loons, mew gulls, bald eagles, tufted puffins, pigeon guillemots and parakeet auklets. Frequented by brown bears. Introduced foxes have died out; introduced ground squirrels thriving.

Sealion Rocks: .008 square miles (5 acres). Glaucous-winged gulls

and at least 2,000 black-legged kittiwakes.

Latax Rocks: .03 square miles (20 acres). Includes rocks, reefs and islets, the largest of which is 8 acres with a peak elevation of 32 feet. Important marine mammal habitat: haul-out for harbor seals, sea otters and Steller sea lions. Nesting black-legged kittiwakes, black oystercatchers, pigeon guillemots, tufted and horned puffins, parakeet auklets. Bears swim to Latax Rocks.

RASPBERRY (map 2):

76.22 square miles; maximum elevation 2,065 feet. Beaver intro-duced in 1924, Sitka black-tailed deer established in the 1960s; also has muskrat, red squirrel and elk.

WHALE (map 2):

13.98 square miles; maximum elevation 2,028 feet.

MARMOT (map 2):

17.4 square miles; maximum elev-ation South Peak (1,262 feet). Site of world's second largest Steller sea lion rookery. Island designated a Special Use Area by state of Alaska.

SPRUCE (map 2):

16.55 square miles; maximum elevation 1,623 feet. Dense Sitka spruce forests. Brown bears, short-tailed weasels, tundra voles and little brown bats native; ground squirrels, red squirrels, Norway rats, beaver and muskrat successfully introduced.

KODIAK (map 3):

3,620 square miles; highest peaks are Koniag (4,470 feet) and Mount Glottof (4,405 feet). Largest island in Alaska and second largest in United States, exceeded only by Hawaii.

Kodiak National Wildlife Refuge, created 1941 for Kodiak brown bears, covers about two-thirds of island. Steller sea lion haul-out at Cape Chiniak.

Fort Abercrombie State Historical Park, Buskin River State Recreation Site and Pasagshak River State Park accessible by road.

UGAK (map 3):

2.4 square miles (1,433 acres); maximum elevation 1,000 feet. Harbor seal haul-out.

TWO HEADED (map 3):

2.9 square miles (1,856 acres); maximum elevation 1,837 feet. Steller sea lion haul-out.

GEESE ISLANDS (map 3):

Gosling: .1 square miles (61 acres); maximum elevation 60 feet.

Gander: .27 square miles (172 acres); maximum elevation 140 feet.

Geese 2: .24 square miles (156 acres); maximum elevation 100 feet.

SITKALIDAK (map 3):

116.4 square miles (third largest island in archipelago; maximum elevation 2,066 feet. Steller sea lion haul-out at Cape Barnabus.

AIAKTALIK (map 3):

7 square miles (4,480 acres); maximum elevation 210 feet. At one time known as Goose Island. Harbor seal haul-out.

SUNDSTRUM (map 3):

.44 square miles (280 acres); maximum elevation 107 feet.

AKHIOK (map 3):

.67 square miles (430 acres); maximum elevation 193 feet. Previously called Round Island.

AMOOK (map 3):

12.45 square miles; maximum elevation 1,646 feet.

UGANIK (map 3):

57.2 square miles, maximum elevation 2,043 feet. Entire island part of Kodiak National Wildlife Refuge.

OTHER ISLANDS IN UGANIK BAY (inset, map 3):

Mostly low and rolling, with alder, some cottonwoods and birch. Sitka black-tailed deer, red fox, snowshoe hare and bald eagles found on most islands; gulls and eiders nest on smaller islets. Area residents use islands for deer hunting, trapping and berry picking.

Sally: 2.44 square miles (1,560 acres); maximum elevation 1,000 feet. Brown bears sometimes swim from Sally to smaller islands.

Sheep: .125 square miles (80 acres); abandoned cabin and docks located here.

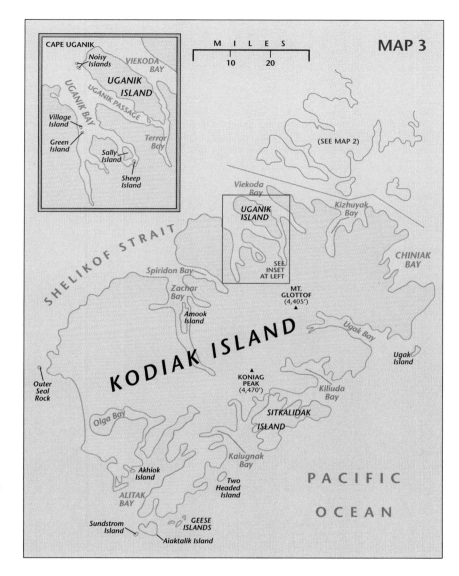

Noisy: .06 square miles (40 acres). Coast Guard light on west shore.

Village: .09 square miles (55 acres); house and outbuildings occupied most of the year.

Green (island and islets): .15 square miles (95 acres).

OUTER SEAL ROCK (map 3):

Pinnacle near Cape Ikolik; Steller sea lion haul-out.

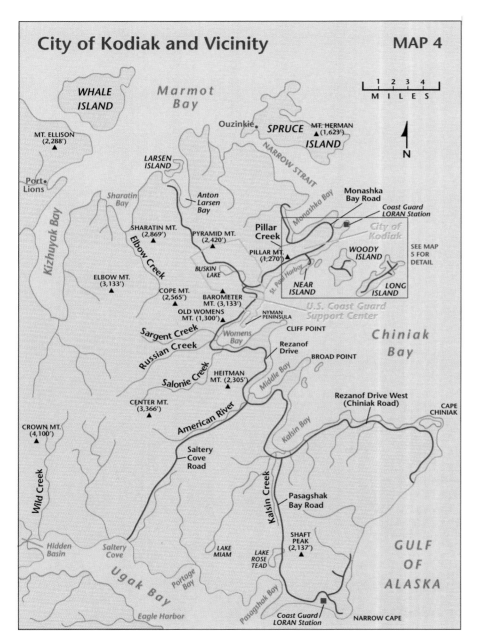

City of Kodiak and Vicinity · MAP 4

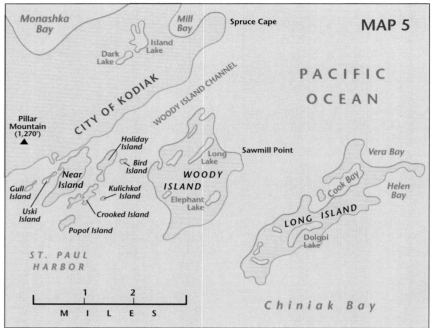

MAP 5

"URBAN ISLANDS" OF THE CITY OF KODIAK (maps 4 and 5):

Near: .44 square miles (280 acres); maximum elevation about 150 feet. Connected by bridge to Kodiak Island.

Popof: .05 square miles (33 acres).

Crooked: .08 square miles (51 acres).

Holiday: .13 square miles (83 acres).

Bird: .01 square miles (7 acres).

Kulichkof: .0003 square miles (.2 acres)

Gull: .014 square miles (9 acres).

Uski: .01 square miles (7 acres).

Long: 1.88 square miles (1,202 acres); maximum elevation 213 feet. Steller sea lion haul-out.

Woody: 2.7 square miles (1.736 acres); maximum elevation 203 feet. Land owners include Women's American Baptist Home Mission; Leisnoi Inc. (Kodiak Native village corporation); several individuals.

Island is thought to have been used by the Russians as an agricultural colony as early as 1792; first horses in Alaska brought here by the Russians; the first road in Alaska built around the island to exercise the horses. Island now has two year-round residents. Baptist mission maintains beef herd and runs summer children's camp.

TRINITY ISLANDS (map 6):

Sitkinak: 64.9 square miles; maximum elevation 1,640 feet at Sitkinak Dome. Steller sea lion haul-out at Cape Sitkinak; harbor seals on beaches to south. Landing strip near Mark Lake; used for cattle ranching.

Tugidak: 65.57 square miles; maximum elevation 161 feet. Designated "Critical Habitat" because of populations of seabirds, waterfowl, wading birds, bald eagles and harbor seals. Extensive tidal flats form lagoon at eastern end off Tugidak Passage; lagoon's eelgrass beds sustain waterfowl, including brant, while staging before fall migration. Of 56 species of birds observed on island, 38 nest here including bald eagles, ducks, swans, willow ptarmigan, passerines, and two colonies of gulls. Sea ducks overwinter here. River otters are only land predator. Harbor seal populations have historically been

as high as 15,000 to 20,000, with as many as 5,500 pups born annually, but in the 1990s harbor seal populations have declined to one-tenth their former numbers.

CHIRIKOF (map 7):

51 square miles (32,640 acres); maximum elevation about 600 feet. Steller sea lion rookery. Harbor seals. Six pink salmon streams. Heavily grazed through the years by cattle and horses.

SEMIDI ISLANDS (map 7):

These nine islands, forming the southern boundary of Kodiak Island Borough, are part of the Alaska Maritime National Wildlife Refuge, Alaska Peninsula Unit, and support breeding populations of seabirds numbering more than 2.4 million. The Semidis' population of more than 1 million breeding murres is exceeded only in the Pribilofs. The

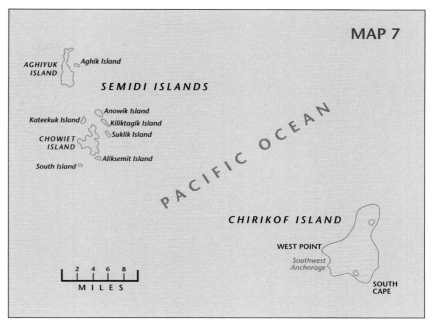

islands have about one-quarter of Alaska's population of northern fulmars. Foxes introduced on larger islands in the 1880s have died off naturally.

Aghiyuk: 5.28 square miles (3,380 acres); maximum elevation 1,024 feet. Seabird populations of more than 500,000; large concentration of murres.

Aghik: .125 square miles (80 acres); maximum elevation 528 feet.

Anowik: .63 square miles (405 acres); maximum elevation 600 feet.

Kaliktagik: .36 square miles (230 acres); maximum elevation 404 feet. Breeding population of Aleutian Canada geese.

Suklik: .18 square miles (75 acres); maximum elevation 345 feet. Thought to have the world's largest nesting colony of horned puffins at about 370,000 birds.

Chowiet: 5.57 square miles (3,565 acres); maximum elevation 679 feet. Steller sea lion rookery. Red-faced and pelagic cormorants, parakeet auklets, least auklets. Rhinoceros auklets found here near the western end of their range.

Aliksemit: .07 square miles (45 acres); maximum elevation 300 feet.

South: Rock, elevation 260 feet.

Kateekuk: .43 square miles (275 acres); maximum elevation 509 feet.

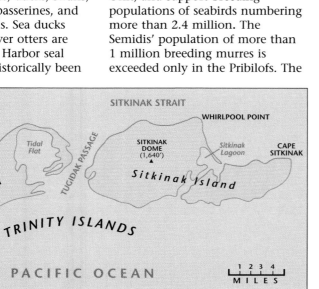

The Communities of Kodiak

Editor's note: *Population figures are from the 1990 federal census and 1991 state-certified borough census. Other sources include the Alaska Department of Community and Regional Affairs and the Kodiak Area Native Association.*

Kodiak Island and its neighbors encompass some 7,500 square miles of upland, much of which is wilderness, difficult to reach and devoid of people. About 90 percent of the Kodiak Island Borough's 15,535 people are concentrated on Kodiak Island's northeast corner, along the road system: 7,229 people in the City of Kodiak, 2,129 on the U.S. Coast Guard base, 150 in Chiniak and 843 in the Bell's Flat area of Women's Bay and another 3,500 in the Spruce Cape and Monashka

Ouzinkie, population 209, lies nestled among the spruce on the west side of Spruce Island. The community got its start as a retirement retreat for Russian American Co. employees. Current residents look to logging, various aspects of fishing, operation of a cold storage facility and tourism for their livelihood. (Marion Stirrup)

Bay areas. About 13 percent of Kodiak town's population is Native.

Another 1,000 or so people, mostly Natives, live in six villages around the edge of Kodiak Island and on Spruce Island. None of these villages are connected by roads to each other or the main town of Kodiak, but all have regularly scheduled air service. The villages have water and sewer services, lights and telephones, post offices, health clinics and borough-run schools.

The borough's remaining 600 or so people live in logging and cannery camps and other remote communities, wilderness lodges and private cabins scattered about the islands.

Here is a quick look at places where people live year-round on Kodiak Island and its neighbors.

THE VILLAGES

In early times, perhaps as early as 6,000 or 7,000 years ago, Kodiak Island was one of the most densely populated places in Alaska. Evidence indicates that thousands of seminomadic Natives lived in dozens of villages and camps, located mostly along rivers, bays and the coasts of Kodiak and its

Old Glory waves over Old Harbor during Fourth of July. (Marion Stirrup)

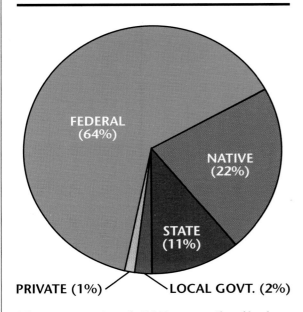
larger neighbors. When the Russians first visited Kodiak Island around 1763, they estimated its population as high as 50,000. While that number may have been exaggerated, contemporary experts believe that the indigenous inhabitants of the Kodiak archipelago, the Koniags, were the most numerous of all Pacific Eskimo groups.

Their numbers fell quickly after contact with foreigners, from warfare and conquest but mostly from New World diseases like smallpox, whooping cough, typhoid and influenza to which the islanders had no immunities. By 1803, the inhabitants of Kodiak and its nearest neighbors were estimated at about 7,000 and 35 years later, their numbers had dropped to about 4,300. By 1844, the 65 Koniag settlements on Kodiak had been consolidated by the Russian American Co. to about seven. In the 1900s, two villages — Aiaktalik and Kanatakvit — were abandoned.

In 1964, following the devastating Good Friday earthquake, Kodiak villagers regrouped once again. The quake, at 8.4 on the Richter scale, was the most violent recorded shake in North America and was felt throughout 500,000 square miles. It generated a series of seismic sea waves that destroyed Old Harbor and Kaguyak on Kodiak Island, Afognak village on Afognak Island, and several settlements on the Alaska Peninsula in an area now within the Kodiak Island Borough. Old Harbor was rebuilt near its former location. Kaguyak, the smallest Kodiak village, was not; two of its 38 residents died in the waves, and most of the rest relocated to Akhiok with some going to Old Harbor. Afognak villagers moved to a new town on Kodiak Island. They named it Port Lions in honor of Lions International.

In 1971, with passage of the Alaska Native Claims Settlement Act (ANCSA), village corporations and one regional corporation, Koniag, Inc., were established to receive land entitlements. Tribal village councils in each village administer a variety of federal programs, many of which are provided by the Kodiak Area Native Association, the nonprofit regional corporation.

These are today's six villages — five on Kodiak Island and one on Spruce Island.

CITY OF OUZINKIE

Ouzinkie (yu-senk-e), population 209, is nestled among tall Sitka spruce in a small cove off Narrow Strait on the west coast of Spruce Island. Narrow Strait separates Spruce Island from Kodiak Island. The village name is a transliteration of Uzenkiy, which is derived from Uskiy, Russian for very narrow.

The town originally was settled as a retirement community for the Russian American Co. The Russian Orthodox monk Father Herman, one of the original members of the Russian spiritual mission, lived here and was buried on the south end of the island, at the shrine at Monk's Lagoon.

In 1890, the Russian Orthodox Church was built, and six years later the Baptist Mission was established. A post office came to Ouzinkie in 1927.

Canneries played prominently in Ouzinkie's early years. In 1889, the Royal Packing Co. constructed the first cannery, and shortly afterward, the American Russian Packing Co. built a second. Others came and went, including the Ouzinkie Packing Co. that was destroyed in the 1964 earthquake. The town has not had a cannery since 1976, when the Glacier Bay cannery burned.

Ouzinkie's population is about 85 percent Native; many of its people are of Russian and Scandinavian descent. The Ouzinkie Village Corp. owns the store and fuel distributorship. The town's economy is based on commercial fishing, with a dozen or so seiners and gillnetters homeported here. Oil from the *Exxon Valdez* spill saturated Ouzinkie's beaches in 1989, closed down fishing and subsistence beach harvesting for that year; three years later, some residents are reluctant to harvest shore foods like clams.

The village corporation makes most of its money from logging, and since 1987 has paid out about $30,000 per shareholder in dividends. About 30,000 acres of the corporation's 115,200-acre entitlement under ANCSA is timbered lands on Afognak Island. The tribal council operates a cold storage facility in Ouzinkie and in 1992 was starting to produce smoked salmon for sale. The village corporation, in cooperation with the state and the Kodiak Regional Aquaculture Association, planned in 1992 to begin stocking 12 streams on Spruce Island with red, silver and king salmon. The village corporation plans to build a sport fishing lodge in 1993, and later others on Afognak and at Anton Larsen Bay, Kodiak. "Recreation is the thing of the future," says William Andy Anderson, corporation president.

CITY OF PORT LIONS

Port Lions, population 222, is located on Settlers Cove, near the mouth of Kizhuyak Bay, on the north coast of Kodiak Island. The land around it varies from Sitka spruce on the north to high brush and grasses on the south. Mixed among the spruce are alder, willow, devil's club, fescue grasses, lupine, ferns and sedges.

The town was founded in 1964 by Lions International, the Bureau of Indian Affairs and the Public Health Service for the displaced inhabitants of Afognak. Afognak had been one of 10 permanent settlements founded by Russian American Co. employees between 1770 and 1799.

For many years, Port Lions was the site of the large Wakefield Cannery on Peregrebni

Point. The cannery burned down in March 1975. The village corporation then purchased a 149-foot floating processor, the *Smokwa*, which processed crab through 1977, generating a couple of dozen local jobs. In 1978, *Smokwa* was sold and moved to Danger Bay, Afognak Island. The *Smokwa/Shell* returned briefly to process king crab in fall and winter 1980, then left the area. The *All Alaskan* processed Tanner crab in Port Lions that year, also.

Although there are no seafood processing facilities here currently, the town's economy is still heavily tied to commercial fishing. A dozen or more boats homeport here, and in the summer several dozen fishing boats are stationed in the area.

Until 1976, a small sawmill operated south of town, but now the buildings are

When the 1964 earthquake destroyed the village of Afognak, residents moved to a new site near Kizhuyak Bay with the help of Lions International. In recognition of that help, the residents named their new community Port Lions. (Marion Stirrup)

vacant. Port Lions has several businesses, including two lodges, a cafe and a general store. Its residents depend to some degree on fishing and hunting for food.

Port Lions has the lowest Native population, about 68 percent, of any of the villages. Its village corporation, Afognak Native Corp., was entitled under ANCSA to select 92,160 acres of federal land; its main business is logging on Afognak Island. In 1992, the Native corporation was trying to sell 150,000 acres on the north side of

Afognak back to the federal government to avoid clearcutting all its entitlement.

With the exception of Kodiak town, Port Lions is the only Kodiak Island village served by the state ferry system.

CITY OF OLD HARBOR

Old Harbor, population 284, is located on Sitkalidak Strait on the southeast coast of Kodiak Island. Vegetation encircling the town, which lines the beach at the foot of a steep mountain, ranges from high brush to

Southernmost of the outlying settlements on Kodiak Island is Akhiok, population 77. Originally a sea otter hunting village, today's residents depend on commercial fishing and subsistence. Wards Cove Packing Co. operates a cannery at Lazy Bay, not far from the village. (George Matz)

alpine tundra. Plants include willow, alder, devil's club, bluejoint and fescue grasses, lupine, Jacob's ladder, ferns, sedges and horsetail.

The area around Old Harbor is thought to have been inhabited for nearly 2,000 years. One of the earliest Russian settlements in Alaska, Three Saints Bay, was located nearby. A description of Old Harbor from 1890 said "Starui Gavan by the Russians and Nunamiut (the land people) by the natives... was once an important station of the Russian fur company, who here obtained large quantities of dried fish for native hunting parties as well as beef for their other employees from herds of cattle which found abundant pasture throughout the year...."

The Old Harbor post office was established in 1931. The town was nearly destroyed by a tidal wave from the 1964

Good Friday earthquake; only two homes and the church remained standing. Old Harbor since has been rebuilt in about same location. The community now has three distinct parts connected by a mile-long road. The downtown includes residents, school, city offices, clinic, church, stores and a restaurant built shortly after the earthquake. Newer residences on a series of hilly streets make up the "uptown" area to the north; the newest section of town is to the northeast.

Many of Old Harbor's residents are commercial fishermen. There are about 32 fishing boats in Old Harbor year-round, and up to 100 during the fishing season. Most of the town's residents depend to some extent on subsistence fishing, hunting and gathering.

There once was a fish processing plant on the floating freezer *Sonya* anchored here, but since this plant burned in 1975, Old Harbor has had no cannery.

The community's population is almost 89 percent Native. The Old Harbor Native Corp., the village corporation, was entitled to 115,200 acres of federal land under ANCSA. It merged with the regional corporation in 1980; four years later it pulled out and reorganized.

CITY OF AKHIOK

This small Native town, population 77, is the most remote village on Kodiak Island. It is located on the south end of the island, about 40 minutes by seaplane from the town of Kodiak. Akhiok sits on Alitak Bay between Kempff and Akhiok bays, in an area dominated by moist tundra with no tall brush or trees.

The original village was located near

Getting There

Two airlines regularly travel between Kodiak and Anchorage, together offering about a dozen regularly scheduled flights a day. Kodiak is about 255 air miles from Anchorage, which translates to a flight of about 45 minutes. Round-trip air fares in 1992 ranged between $170 to $300, with discounted commuter coupons available for a bit less.

MarkAir flies passenger and freight five times a day during the week, with four flights a day on the weekends. For its Kodiak service, MarkAir uses 737 jets and Dash 8s.

Era Aviation Inc. operates daily commuter service in partnership with Alaska Airlines from Anchorage. Era also offers freight service and small package express. The company flies Convair 580s, 50-seat twin-engine turbo-props, and Dash 8s, 37-seat twin-engine prop planes. Alaska Airlines added 737 jet service in August 1992. Era also offers charter helicopter service out of Kodiak.

Also providing transportation between Kodiak and the mainland is the Alaska State Ferry System's *Tustumena*. Direct connections are available weekly through the summer out of Homer or Seward, and the trip to Kodiak across Shelikof Strait takes about 12 hours. The ferry also runs from Kodiak to Port Lions, a two-hour trip. Service is less frequent during the winter. About once a month during summer, the *Tustumena* continues from Kodiak to Dutch Harbor with stops along the Alaska Peninsula. Vehicle and passenger reservations, with or without sleeping berths, are available. Fares in 1992 started at $46 a person one-way from Homer, with discounts for senior citizens and children ages 6-12. Kids under 6 travel free.

Camping sites and trailer hookups on the Kodiak road system can be found at private campgrounds; the city-owned Sandy Beach Park; and Buskin State Park and Fort Abercrombie State Park.

Car rentals are available from several outlets. In 1992, Kodiak's single taxi company charged about $14 for a one-way ride from the airport to downtown.

Freight comes to the island on both passenger and cargo air carriers. Waterborne shipments arrive on Samson Tug and Barge Service and Sea-Land Freight. Overnight, express mail and freight deliveries are provided by several fast freight services.

A number of air taxis and charter companies operate out of Kodiak, providing passenger, mail and freight service to villages and remote destinations, such as park service and private cabins, as well as flightseeing, wildlife viewing and dropoffs for hunting and fishing. The borough's six villages — Ouzinkie, Port Lions, Old Harbor, Akhiok, Karluk and Larsen Bay — are regularly served by two air companies about five times a day, weather permitting. Air fare to the villages on scheduled flights ranges from $30 to $75 one way. Charter rates are based on flying time and plane size, and range from $160 an hour to $525 an hour.

A number of charter boat

Several airlines including MarkAir and Era Aviation fly to Kodiak from Anchorage. For those who prefer water travel, the ferry Tustumena *calls at Kodiak and Port Lions. (Matt Johnson)*

companies offer excursions into the ocean playground around Kodiak. Fishing, wildlife viewing and diving charters, along with water taxis to remote sites are among the services offered. Costs vary and a certain amount of dockside dickering is not unusual, but base rates range from $75 a half-day to $175 a full day, including tackle for fishing. The Kodiak Island Charter Vessel Owners Association, formed by nine companies in winter 1991, acts as a clearinghouse for charter boat information and offers a central booking service, particularly useful when arranging large group charters. There are other companies, not part of the vessel owners association as of 1991, who also book charters.

Numerous wilderness lodges offer hunting, fishing and sightseeing packages that include lodging and usually transportation. Other lodges are located along Kodiak's road system. Finally, there are a number of fishing and bear hunting camps located in remote areas.

Larsen Bay is the only Kodiak Island outlying settlement with an active cannery. Alaska Packers Association began operating their cannery here in 1911; today Kodiak Salmon Packers employs about 160 seasonally in this community with a year-round population of 147. (Roz Goodman)

Humpy Cove. The area first appeared in written history in 1763, when Russian explorer Stepan Glotov reported landing nearby. The name Akhiok first was reported in the 1880 census. A post office operated here from 1933 to 1945 and reopened in 1964. During the 1930s and World War II, the village was renamed Alitak by the postal service to avoid confusion with a village near Bethel in western Alaska named Akiak. The name later was changed back to Akhiok.

The community originally was a sea otter hunting settlement. Today, fishing supports the economy. Although there are no commercial fishing facilities in Akhiok, a cannery is located five miles south, on Lazy Bay.

A oyster-culture pilot project started here September 1991, under direction of the Kodiak Area Native Association. KANA hopes to develop oyster culture into a new economy for the villages. The 100,000 oysters, from seed stock bought out of California, Washington or British Columbia, are kept in nets on long lines and tended by Akhiok villagers. Though the water is colder than in conventional oyster-growing areas such as along the Washington coast, it is also extremely productive. The suspension technique allows the animals to feed constantly and their growth rates have been surprisingly high. According to Mark Donohue, mariculturist with the Kodiak Area Native Association, the long-term outlook for oyster farming in Alaska looks promising. Oyster beds elsewhere such as in Maryland's Chesapeake Bay and the Gulf of Mexico are being closed because of pollution. Once beds are contaminated, according to Donohue, it takes a long time to turn them around. Oysters from the Akhiok project should be ready for harvest in spring 1993, and will be marketed to restaurants to serve on the half-shell.

Most of Akhiok's residents, 93.5 percent, are Native. Almost all of Akhiok's people rely on subsistence fishing and hunting — salmon, crab, shrimp, clam, duck, seal, deer, rabbit and bear — for food. The town's only general store closed in 1975.

The Akhiok-Kaguyak Village Corp. was entitled under ANCSA to slightly more than 138,000 acres of federal land. In December 1980, the village corporation merged with Koniag, Inc., the regional corporation, but later pulled out.

VILLAGE OF KARLUK

The isolated village of Karluk, population 71, is located on the west coast of Kodiak Island, on storm-ridden Shelikof Strait.

Prior to 1978, the village was located on each side of the Karluk River, in the area of Karluk Lagoon. A spit and a foot bridge connected Old Karluk, on the northeast side of the lagoon, with Karluk on the southwest side. In January 1978, northeasterly winds reaching 100 miles an hour took out the bridge. Most of the families moved to new homes built about a mile up the lagoon, although a few residents stayed at the old town. A gravel airstrip is located between the two areas.

Karluk sits amid low brush, high brush and moist tundra. Scattered patches of willow and alder mix with sedges, rushes, lichens, cottongrass, cranberry, crowberry and blueberry, along with bluejoint, fescue and beach rye grasses, fireweed, ferns and dwarf birch.

In 1784, Russian hunters wintered at Karluk; two years later they established a trading post. However, the mouth of Karluk River is thought to have been populated for at least 5,000 years before the Russians arrived on Kodiak Island. Between 1790 and 1850 many tanneries, salteries and canneries were established in the area. By the late 1880s, Karluk was reknown for having one of the largest salmon fisheries in Alaska, and the river was known as the greatest red salmon stream in the world.

A post office was established in 1892. In the early 1900s, canneries were constructed by the Alaska Packers Association. Over-fishing of the area forced the canneries to close in the 1930s, and today the buildings stand vacant, in deteriorating condition.

Karluk's population is 91.5 percent

Native. Hunting and fishing provides a substantial part of the villagers' food. The village is unincorporated. The Karluk Native Corp. was entitled to receive 92,160 acres of federal land under ANCSA. In December 1980, the village corporation merged with the regional corporation, Koniag Inc.

CITY OF LARSEN BAY

The community of Larsen Bay, population 147, is located near the mouth of Larsen Bay, on the west shore of Uyak Bay, on the northwest corner of Kodiak Island. This is an area of high brush with scattered Sitka spruce, along with alder, willow, devil's club, grasses, lupine, ferns, sedges and horsetail.

The bay was named for Peter Larsen, a furrier, hunter and guide from Unga Island in the Shumagins. The Native name for the town is Uyak. The area is thought to have been inhabited for 2,000 years by the Koniag people. In certain sections of the community, hundreds of prehistoric artifacts have been uncovered. In the early 1800s, there was a tannery in Uyak Bay. Alaska Packers Association built a cannery in the village of Larsen Bay in 1911. The cannery is now operated by Kodiak Salmon Packers.

Larsen Bay is definitely a fishing community. It is the only Kodiak Island village with a cannery, which brings an influx of outsiders to the village each summer. The cannery employs about 160 workers, mostly college students. It buys salmon from a few local setnetters and from a dozen tenders that service the 100 or so purse seiners that fish Larsen Bay area waters.

Outside the cannery, the few local jobs are mostly with the local government and tribal council. Many residents depend on subsistence harvest of fish and game, such as seal, salmon, halibut, codfish, clams, sea urchins, crab, deer and berries. About 84 percent of Larsen Bay's population is Native. Its village corporation, Nu-Nachk Pit, was entitled to select 115,200 acres of federal land under ANCSA. In 1980 the village corporation merged with Koniag, Inc.

LOGGING CAMPS

A couple of hundred people live in two logging camps at Danger Bay on Afognak Island. The Ben Thomas Camp — with a collection of trailers and wooden buildings serving as family residences, bunkhouses, offices, a mess hall and school — logs for Afognak Native Corp. and Afognak Joint Venture. The Silver Bay logging camp works for Koncor Forest Products, a joint venture of four village corporations: Ouzinkie Corp., Natives of Kodiak, Chenega and Yakutat.

OLD BELIEVERS VILLAGE

Afognak Island also is home to a relatively new Russian Old Believer's community. The settlement on the southern tip of Afognak, near the entrance to Raspberry Strait from Whale Pass, was established about 1989 by families splintered from the Old Believer's group near Kachemak Bay on the Kenai Peninsula. Operating as Aleneva Joint Ventures, they bought 240 acres of Native allotments through the Bureau of Indian Affairs. Seven families were reported living there in 1992.

ELSEWHERE AROUND THE BOROUGH

Large remote communities on Kodiak Island include the two Wards Cove canneries, at Port Bailey and at Lazy Bay. Each have about 100 people throughout the summer.

Other year-round remote residents include the Wayne McCrary family on Chirikof Island, who are caretakers for a grazing lease. They get groceries and mail delivered about once a month by floatplane, weather permitting. Others live off the land, trapping, fishing and hunting, in places such as Tugidak Island, Hidden Basin, Hermit Cove, Amook Island, and Iron Creek in Raspberry Strait. A group of five or more families who live in the Village Islands on the southwest side of Uganik Bay comprise one of the larger remote communities. Other year-round residents include caretakers of quite a few wilderness lodges in locations like Seal Bay on north Afognak, Port Williams on Shuyak and Selief Bay in Raspberry Strait.

Aqua-roofed Karluk Lodge looks out over a portion of Karluk, population 77, smallest of the Kodiak Island villages. The main part of town is across the river. (Don Pitcher)

Prehistory of the Kodiak Archipelago

BY RICK KNECHT

Editor's note: *Rick Knecht is an archaeologist and coordinator of the Culture & Heritage Program for the Kodiak Area Native Association.*

In the prehistoric past, as today, the economy of Kodiak Island depended on the resources of the sea. Currents upwelling from offshore depths supply minerals and nutrients, forming the foundation for one of the world's most productive marine ecosystems. For Native settlers arriving in the North Pacific shortly after the retreat of glacial ice, this abundance nurtured some

In 1991, the Smithsonian Institution returned human bones and artifacts taken by Ales Hrdlicka in the 1930s from Larsen Bay. A Russian Orthodox priest leads the reburial service for 370 cardboard boxes containing remains of 756 people, some 2,000 years old. The repatriation came after a five-year legal fight by the Larsen Bay Tribal Council and the Native American Rights Fund, which resulted in passage in 1990 of a federal law that gives Natives the right to their ancestors' remains held in museums. (Marion Stirrup)

of the largest populations of prehistoric Alaska, and fostered development of a rich and complex series of cultures.

Archaeological sites on Kodiak Island are numerous. More than 700 sites, mostly prehistoric villages, have been documented on the archipelago; hundreds of miles of shoreline are yet to be investigated by archaeologists. Middens, composed of layers of prehistoric food refuse and house remains, frequently reach 12 feet or more in depth. Larger village sites can extend along salmon streams and protected inlets for more than a mile. Remains of former dwellings in the form of housepit depressions as old as 2,000 years are still visible on the ground surface.

The cool maritime climate has ensured that preservation conditions are generally good and, in some cases, extraordinary. The remains of prehistoric food refuse in the form of animal bones and shells, bone artifacts and human remains have been recovered from sites dating back more than 6,000 years. Water-saturated soils on some sites have occasionally prevented decay processes by sealing off oxygen. Wood, hide,

This 1,000-year-old hearth made from slate slabs was typical of houses on the archipelago 1,000 to 2,000 years ago. These hearths were centrally located inside semisubterranean dwellings, and used for cooking and heating. (Rick Knecht)

Archaeologist Rick Knecht, 39, spends summers mapping and exploring ancient village sites of the Kodiak archipelago. Erosion and vandalism are taking a toll. "We're in a race against time. We're struggling to get a basic inventory of thousands of miles of coastline," says Knecht, who works for the Kodiak Area Native Association. Philomena Knecht, a linguist and Alutiiq curriculum specialist for KANA, often joins her husband in the field. In 1992, Philomena implemented an Alutiiq language emersion program at Kodiak High School and Old Harbor and Akhiok village schools, funded with an $80,000 federal education grant. (Marion Stirrup)

fur, feathers, baleen, spruce root and other fragile organic artifacts have been found nearly perfectly preserved on sites dating back to A.D. 1,200.

In addition to village sites, ancient stone weirs in salmon streams, petroglyphs of men and animals, burial caves, stone cairns, boulder arrangements, chert quarries, deeply worn trails and fortified sea stacks provide tantalizing clues to Kodiak Island's past. Kodiak's cultural heritage is a complex story, one that archaeologists are only just beginning to understand.

OCEAN BAY: AN EARLY MARITIME CULTURE

Kodiak Island's earliest reliably dated sites were occupied around 6,500 years ago. Archaeologist Donald Clark discovered the first remains from this early culture near Ocean Bay, on Sitkalidak Island, in 1962. Since that time, Ocean Bay sites have been found at various locations around Kodiak Island, as well as on the adjacent shore of the Alaska Peninsula. Recent geological work has determined that tectonic forces have sometimes lifted sections of Kodiak's coastline. Former shoreline terraces have been left far inland as lagoons and bays were drained by the gradual uplift. Several well-preserved Ocean Bay sites have been subsequently discovered on these fossil shorelines.

Housefloors of Ocean Bay peoples are vividly defined by thin layers of bright red ocher, recovered from mineral deposits and powdered with heavy stone grinders. The earliest dwellings appear to be tentlike structures, probably constructed from sea mammal hides over a wooden frame. By 5,000 B.P., semisubterranean sod dwellings

also appear, possibly used on a seasonal basis. The earliest Ocean Bay knives and projectile points were most often made from chipped stone. Later tool kits, dating from about 5,000 years ago, show an increasing preference for lance tips and flensing knives made by grinding and sharpening slate.

Recent discoveries by Harvard University archaeologist Philomena Knecht at the Rice Ridge site, near Chiniak, have confirmed that Ocean Bay peoples were accomplished maritime hunters and fishermen. According to preliminary studies of well-preserved animal bones recovered from this site, marine resources have been remarkably stable for the last six millennia. Composite bone fish hooks and grooved cobbles were used in deep sea fishing for cod and halibut. Animal bones include those of large sea lions, seals, sea otters and whales. Shellfish remains including blue mussel, butter clams, chitons, limpets and sea urchins are also abundant. Bilaterally barbed bone harpoons with twin line guards are reminiscent of forms recovered from early sites in coastal British Columbia. Woodworking tools, awls, needles, pendants and other bone and ivory items were also found.

Two fragmentary human remains, the oldest ever found in Alaska, have dental characteristics that fall in the range of variation typical of modern Eskimos and Aleuts, although the sample is too small to determine the ethnic affiliation of Ocean Bay peoples with certainty. However, the presence of ground stone oil lamps may well indicate that Ocean Bay settlers were the ancestors of Aleut-Eskimo peoples who inhabit the region today.

Tools and chipping waste of stone from

the Alaska Peninsula, as well as caribou and other animal bones not native to Kodiak Island, indicate that the Ocean Bay peoples possessed sufficient watercraft and skills to routinely traverse 30-mile-wide Shelikof Strait to the Alaska mainland.

KACHEMAK PHASE:
RISING POPULATIONS AND DIVERSITY

The transitional states leading from the Ocean Bay to the Kachemak phase, which had occurred by 2,500 years ago, are not well documented. Only one Kodiak Island site has thus far dated from this time period, and on the Alaska Peninsula no sites have been found from the time period ranging from 2,800 to 1,800 years B.P. Kachemak phase sites were first described by Frederica de Laguna, who began excavating in the Kachemak Bay area of Cook Inlet in 1930.

In some long-occupied sites, such as near Karluk Lagoon, 16 inches of weathered volcanic ash, generated by volcanoes on the Alaska Peninsula, separate the Ocean Bay layers from Kachemak strata. It is possible that a period of active volcanism resulted in a smaller, less archaeologically visible population.

Kachemak phase sites were often intensively occupied for long periods of time, as evidenced by deep middens of shell-fish and sea mammal bones. Houses were semisubterranean, single-roomed structures, sometimes with small storage alcoves on one or more corners. Clay-lined pits, perhaps used to store fish and other food, are found in Kachemak dwellings. Floor plans of Kachemak dwellings are closely similar in size and form within sites, suggesting that Kachemak society may have been relatively

BELOW: *Karluk One, a rare "wet" site with water-saturated soils that protect artifacts from oxygen and decay, has yielded numerous fragile items still intact despite their age, like these 500-year-old salmon bones. Such discoveries provide insights into prehistoric diet and lifeways. In 1992, exploration began of a newly discovered wet site, Nuniliak, on Afognak Island. Few wet sites are known in North America. (Rick Knecht)*

RIGHT: *Thousands of items found in an ancient village site, known as Karluk One near the modern village of Karluk, help explain life of early Koniags. This cottonwood bark ceremonial mask, from 200 to 800 years old, is one of many wooden items uncovered here. (Ben Fitzhugh, courtesy of Rick Knecht)*

LOWER RIGHT: *This 600-year-old spruce root basket, from Karluk One, shows the fine craftsmanship used in even the most utilitarian objects. This basket-making technique is still used on Kodiak and in southeastern Alaska. (Rick Knecht)*

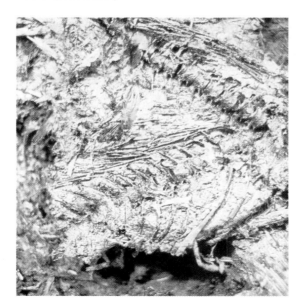

ABOVE: *This cutaway at Crag Point, between Anton Larsen and Sharatin bays, shows layers of material accumulated through about 2,000 years of continuous occupation. (Rick Knecht)*

RIGHT: *More than 700 archaeological sites are known in the Kodiak archipelago, evidence that the islands were one of the earliest and most populated regions in Alaska. These volunteers with the Kodiak Area Native Association are excavating a site at Crag Point. (Rick Knecht)*

egalitarian. Houses are often clustered in groups of from one to 40, and sites seem to have been most intensively occupied near overlapping habitats of marine animals.

Amy Steffian of the University of Michigan excavated 16 Kachemak structures at the Uyak site, near the modern village of Larsen Bay. The dwellings featured 18-foot-long entrance tunnels, centrally located slate slab hearths and slightly raised earthen platforms along one or more walls.

While Kachemak phase houseforms and assemblages retain many common features,

stylistic diversity in art and artifacts seems to reach its peak during this time. During late Kachemak times, an increasing number of artifacts and raw materials appear that are exotic to the island, which indicates a likely increase in long-distance trade and contact with neighboring groups elsewhere in coastal Alaska. Lip plugs or labrets, beads and similar decorative items were made from hard coal or jet.

KONIAG PHASE:
THE RISE OF CULTURAL COMPLEXITY

About 800 years ago, houseforms and settlement patterns again began to change. Kodiak Native culture reached perhaps its

most spectacular florescence during this period, which witnessed the rise of even greater populations, long-distance warfare, trade, slavery, ceremonialism and a ranked society based on accumulated wealth and kinship. The semisubterranean sod house, later known by the Russians as a barabara, reached an unprecedented size, averaging about 700 square feet of interior space. Occupied by members of an extended family, a barabara consisted of a large central room, joined by two or more side rooms. Each dwelling housed about 20 people. Settlements along salmon streams like the Karluk and Ayakulik rivers have been found to have from 150 to 170 barabaras. Similarly large villages also existed near prime sea mammal hunting localities.

The Karluk One site near the modern village of Karluk was continuously occupied between A.D. 1,200 and the 18th century. It was excavated by the late Richard Jordan and the author, who found more than 15,000 artifacts, 70 percent of which were made from wood. Spruce-root baskets, weapons, kayak parts, toys, bowls, masks, artwork, tools and other items found at Karluk One have added much to our understanding of the Koniag phase. Although tools of stone, bone and ivory tend to be less ornate and more utilitarian than that of the preceding Kachemak phase, the Koniags were superb craftsmen in wood.

By the last half of the 18th century, Russian fur hunters had begun to find their way to Kodiak, following the sea otters along the Aleutian chain and up the Alaska Peninsula. The first contacts between Kodiak Natives and Europeans probably took place on the south end of Kodiak Island on the

Aiaktalik Peninsula. In 1763, Stepan Glotov made a landfall in Russian Harbor. In summer 1992, a team of archaeologists from the Kodiak Area Native Association located the four large barabaras Glotov encountered and whose residents at the time promptly fled. The Russians repelled subsequent attacks by well-armed and organized Koniag warriors, however attempts to trade for furs were largely unsuccessful. Other attempts by Russian traders to establish a foothold on Kodiak were similarly defeated.

In 1784, Grigorri Shelikov came prepared to defend against Native resistence, and founded Kodiak's first permanent Russian settlement at Three Saints Bay. Days after his ships had anchored, he sent out armed parties of hunters to demand hostages from the Natives.

The key to Russian subjugation of Koniag society was the taking of hostages from ruling families. Children of chiefs were specifically sought, and at times several hundred hostages were held for such purposes at the Three Saints Bay settlement. The fact that the Koniag, so superior in numbers to the Russians, could be held in check through the threat of harm to hostages is strong evidence of the political power possessed by influential families.

Natives at first refused to surrender their children, and gathered on a sea stack near Sitkalidak Island. Sea stacks are steep-walled islets, but often have tops large and level enough to construct barabaras. Stocked with provisions, the stacks were used as a defensive refuge in much the same way as medieval Europeans used castles. Kodiak Area Native Association archaeologists found and excavated the site in 1992, and mapped 28 multiple-room barabara pits and many hearths of temporary shelters on the three-acre rock.

Shelikov stormed the stronghold with the aid of cannon and 70 men armed with muskets. The several thousand Natives who had taken refuge there panicked with the noise and smoke generated by the cannon, and were routed. Hundreds were killed, and hundred more taken captive. The back of the Koniag resistence was broken, and their independence soon ended.

Shelikov claimed that no less than 50,000 Koniag subjects could now be added to the Russian empire, a claim that was probably inflated, but not entirely fantastic. While a population of 50,000 seems improbable, an estimate of 20,000 for Kodiak and the Alaska Peninsula would be reasonable. Introduced diseases, coupled with the abuses of the early fur-hunting system, drastically reduced the Native population during the early years of the 19th century.

As archaeological discoveries reveal increasing numbers of large village sites, estimates of the Koniag population at contact will continue to be revised upward. Today their descendants are rediscovering their ancient past through research and education, and an abiding respect for the traditions and lifeways passed down to them during many generations.

The late Dr. Ales Hrdlicka (white hair and dark suit) supervised several archaeological digs on Kodiak in the 1930s. In 1935 his crew at Uyak included from left: C.B. McKee, G.A. Seib, J. Barton, R.F. Heizer, E.H. Bell, H. Enslow and R.H. Merrill. (Courtesy of Anchorage Museum of History and Art)

Where the Wild Ram Cries

The late 17th century found maritime world powers gripped in exploratory frenzy and as they reached the northern Pacific Ocean, Alaska appeared. The Kodiak archipelago with its abundance of valuable fur-bearing animals enticed England and Spain. However, the Russians claimed the islands first, as they expanded eastward through the Aleutians from Siberia, Kamchatka and the Kuriles.

One of the earliest Russian settlements in America sprang up on Kodiak, at Three Saints Bay. Kodiak Island became the Russian commercial center for hunting and exploration in the North Pacific.

The Russians learned about Kodiak Island, or Kad'aik as it was called, in 1741 when Danish Capt. Vitus Bering sailed by the island during his second Kamchatka expedition to the east for the Russian

In early times, clams and other shellfish were important winter foods. The tradition of harvesting beach foods continues today. These men are collecting blue mussels at Monashka Bay. (Marion Stirrup)

government. Two decades passed, however, before any Russians came ashore on Kodiak.

Stepan Glotov was the first. He landed September 1763 and stayed nine months. He had heard much about Kodiak from the Aleuts on Umnak Island in the Aleutians, where he had wintered on a previous expedition. The Koniags of Kodiak attacked Glotov's ship at least three times. Finally they began trading sea otter, fox and other animal pelts for colored beads, Glotov reported.

Between 1756 and 1780, voyages to America became almost commonplace — 48 expeditions sailed from Russia to the Aleutian Islands and on to the south coast of the Alaska Peninsula and Kodiak Island, according to A.I. Alekseev in *The Destiny of Russian America, 1741-1867* (1990). Several Russian fur hunting vessels after Glotov attempted trade on Kodiak, but hostile Natives spooked them off.

The first Russian settlement on Kodiak was Three Saints Bay, founded by Grigorii Shelikov in 1784. Three Saints is said to be the first permanent Russian post in America, but some scholars now give that distinction

Russian dancers promenade in this scene from "Cry of the Wild Ram," Alaska's longest-running outdoor drama held each August for the past quarter-century at Fort Abercrombie in Kodiak. The play depicts Russian America from 1790 to 1821. In 1993, the play will not be staged so it can be rewritten to address concerns of Natives and the Russian Orthodox Church about the way Natives and the priests are depicted. (Jim Simmen)

Panorama View of Kodiak, Alaska

KODIAK ALASKA 206

These two images show Kodiak at it appeared in the early 1920s (photo at left) and in the 1940s (panorama above). (Both courtesy of Michael Nore)

to Unalaska. Three Saints Bay did give Russia an important stronghold in the New World. In 1792, the settlement was moved to Pavlovsk Harbor, now the town of Kodiak. Even after the governmental headquarters for Russian America moved to Sitka in 1804, Kodiak remained vital to Russian activities along Alaska's coast, as well as a supply base for their expeditions to California and Hawaii.

Shelikov, a shrewd businessman, realized profits lurked in the Alaska fur trade. After dabbling in numerous companies to finance hunting expeditions, he and two other merchants formed their own company with the idea of colonizing Alaska, in addition to gathering furs. He sailed with his family on

the company's first expedition, eventually anchoring in a bay on southeast Kodiak that he named Three Saints after his ship.

Shelikov quickly styled Three Saints Bay as a Russian village, with frame buildings and vegetable gardens. He built a school to teach the Koniags Russian ways, language and religion. He sent groups of Koniag men supervised by Russian traders out to hunt sea otters and survey the coasts of Kodiak, nearby islands and the Alaska Peninsula. Meanwhile, women, children and men unfit for hunting worked for the Russians, drying fish, gathering berries, tending the gardens. Shelikov painted himself as a generous benefactor in his letters, although others said he was cruel to the Natives.

In 1786 he returned to Russia, leaving merchant K. A. Samoilov in charge of the Russian settlements, which by this time included several on Kodiak Island, a fort on Afognak Island and an outpost in Prince William Sound. The next year, he sent E.I. Delarov to replace Samoilov. He also sent some of Kodiak's first domestic livestock — two pairs of vicious dogs for breeding, two pairs of rabbits, two cows, two bulls, two pairs of pigs and a pair of goats.

Russian colonization ignited in 1791, when Alexander Baranov arrived in Kodiak. Shelikov had hounded Baranov to take over the company's American holdings, and the new manager proved himself an enthusiastic expansionist. One of Baranov's first actions was to move Russian headquarters to Kodiak town's present site, after a plague of earthquakes and tidal waves destroyed Three Saints Bay. Baranov's new settlement on Chiniak Bay quickly took shape, with comfortable homes and service buildings. From here he launched hunting and exploration parties. He ventured by bidara around the coast of Kodiak, and sailed numerous times into southeastern Alaska.

He set up a shipbuilding yard in Resurrection Bay, near present-day Seward, and one on Spruce Island near Kodiak.

In fall 1794, a spiritual mission of nine clerics led by Father Ioasaf arrived in Kodiak, along with families for an agricultural colony at Yakutat across the Gulf of Alaska. Baranov and the monks did not get along. He resented their interference; they complained about the heathenly, drunken behavior of Baranov and the Russian fur traders. Some reports indicated the monks were less than saintly themselves. Nevertheless, a Russian Orthodox church with brass bells forged by the colonists went up within two years.

The priests traveled around the region converting Natives. They blessed hunting parties of hundreds of men gathered by the village chiefs. These hunters would be gone an entire season, traveling more than 1,200 miles in one-man bidarkas and the larger

St. Herman

STORY AND PHOTO BY ANDY HALL

During the annual pilgrimage to Spruce Island, Tina Waselie speaks with Archimandrite Innocent on the steps of the S.S. Sergius and Herman of Valaam Chapel built over the former grave of St. Herman.

Father Herman was a member of the original Kodiak Mission sent out from the ancient Valaam Monastery in Russian Finland. The 10 missionaries arrived on Kodiak Island on September 24, 1794; and almost from the moment of their arrival they came into conflict with the fur traders of the Russian American Co. over the treatment of Kodiak's Natives.

In 1800, company manager Alexander Baranov placed the missionaries under house arrest and forbade any contact between them and the Natives. The following year, the missionaries attempted to extend Imperial protection to the Natives by administering to them the oath of allegiance to the Czar. An enraged Baranov threatened the monks with physical violence, which prompted the clerics to retreat into their compound, and to refuse to celebrate church services in public for more than a year.

At an undetermined time, between 1808 and 1818, Father Herman retreated to a small island near Kodiak that he named New Valaam, now called Spruce Island. He lived on the island, caring for orphans, running a school and teaching the Natives. He developed what was probably the first experimental agricultural station and introduced the use of seaweed as fertilizer. Father Herman is credited with miraculous powers including healings, averting natural disasters and prophecies. Among the latter is the withdrawal of Russia from Alaska. Father Herman died on his island in 1837.

On August 9, 1970, after years of preparation, Father Herman was canonized by the Orthodox Church in America. Each year since 1970, pilgrims from around the world gather in Kodiak and on August 9 travel to Spruce Island for a short service to commemorate the canonization of St. Herman.

skin bidaras along the coast, setting up winter quarters wherever they landed. In Baranov's first census of Kodiak Island in 1795, he counted 6,206 people, with as many as 700 bidaras engaged in sea otter hunting. Many Koniag men, despite their excellent boat handling skills, died on these forced hunts because of bad weather and poor diets; their families at home also suffered because after working for the Russians they had little time or energy and no able-bodied men to help stock their own provisions. More than one visitor to the island observed hunger among the Natives during late winter. Clams and other shellfish dug from the beaches near the villages were important winter foods.

In 1799, the Russian government consolidated all the companies operating in America into a big monopoly, the Russian American Co. That same year, Baranov moved the Russian America capital to Sitka and alternated his time between there and Kodiak. The Russian colony suffered a few setbacks — Sitka was attacked by Tlingits in 1802 and had to be retaken, and the first ship built at Resurrection Bay, the *Phoenix*, wrecked on a return voyage with supplies from Russia. Yet Kodiak generally prospered. Alaska's first library and museum started here in 1805. V.M. Golovin visited in 1818 and called Pavlovsk Harbor "the most profitable and best of the company's settlements...fish of the best varieties is caught in unbelievable quantity..." Salteries were established at Karluk and Uyak bays and two brickyards operated on Kodiak and Long islands.

Russian imperialism brought many changes to the Koniag. Their traditional clothing included animal skin parkas, transluscent rain parkas (*kamleikas*) sewn of dried animal intestines, and broad-brimmed grass and woven root hats decorated with shells, sea lion whiskers and painted figures. Both men and women adorned their faces with lip and nose labrets. However, the Russians would not allow them to keep animal pelts for personal use, and they distributed clothing to the Natives from their warehouses. The Russians also resettled the Koniag into larger villages closer to their artels. Natives dwellings, semisubterranean sod barabaras, took on features of Russian buildings, such as wooden doors and square windows. Russians and Natives married, creating a new class of Americans called creoles who were priviledged with social status. Russian lineage can be traced today through modern surnames. The Russian Orthodox mission imprinted a faith still devoutly practiced on Kodiak Island.

By mid-1800s the Russian American Co. was floundering, overextended financially and provisionally. In 1867 Russia sold Alaska to the United States. Many company employees, particularly those who had married into Native families, continued living in Russian settlements on Kodiak, Spruce and Afognak islands. The U.S. Army occupied "Fort Kodiak" since Alaska was considered Indian country lacking a civil government; the military were to protect Natives from unscrupulous settlers, traders, fishermen and other warring tribes. In April 1868, San Francisco merchant H.M. Hutchinson stopped in Kodiak with the last governor of Russian America, Prince D.M. Maksutoff, who transferred the company's holdings to Hutchinson. Prices escalated,

A popular Russian Orthodox tradition is the Christmas "starring" ceremony, shown here at the Holy Resurrection Cathedral in Kodiak. (Marion Stirrup)

One of the earliest Russian settlements in North America sprang up at Three Saints Bay on Kodiak's southeast side. This view looks over Cape Liakik into the mouth of the bay off Sitkalidak Strait. A continuing discussion among Russian America scholars is whether the Russian post at Unalaska predated Three Saints Bay. "It would be interesting to clear it up," says University of Alaska history professor Richard Pierce, who also edits and publishes books about Russian America. (Chlaus Lotscher)

and some people lost their homes and jobs in the transition. The Hutchinson and Kohl Co. eventually became the Alaska Commercial Co., the largest fur operator on Kodiak.

Commerical whaling by New England boats, which had plied Kodiak waters since about 1835, was beginning to play out by the 1870s. Fur trading was still profitable, although the conservation measures instituted by the Russians to maintain healthy sea otter stocks were abandoned by the Americans and the animals were almost extinct by 1890. In 1911, an international treaty finally banned hunting.

Little else was going on during the early American period in Kodiak except ice exports from Woody Island's Tanignak Lake by the San Francisco Ice Co. for sale in California, and stopovers of ships involved in sealing in the Pribilof Islands. During the early years of the American period, more people lived on Woody Island than in the town of Kodiak, and the North American Commercial Co.

opened a fur station to buy sea otter pelts hunted by Woody Island Natives.

About 1903, Otto Kraft, who managed the Woody Island station, opened his own store, O. Kraft & Son, in Kodiak. By this time, Kodiak again percolated with people. The salmon industry boomed with major canneries at the mouth of the Karluk River that enticed hundreds of men north each summer to work on beach crews. The gold rush to Nome brought prospectors through Kodiak en route to the fields. The U.S. Department of Agriculture moved its experiment station and its herd of cattle from Woody Island to Kodiak and Kalsin Bay. The government began operating a wireless station in Kodiak and on Woody Island in 1911.

The eruption of Novarupta volcano in June 1912, however, threw a damper on Kodiak. The mighty discharge veiled the sun for two days and tons of ash piled up 18 inches deep on the flats, burying the land and plants and clogging salmon streams and drinking wells. Ash and sulfur odors hung so thick that a 20-room log building caught fire and burned undetected by people 200 feet away. The U.S. Revenue Cutter *Manning* evacuated hundreds of people, anchoring off Woody Island to wait out the blackness. The vessel's captain, K.W. Perry, visited Kodiak's two saloons shortly after the ash started falling. "...finding considerable drinking," he wrote later, "requested the proprietors to close. This they readily did, agreeing with me that it was a time for every man to keep his mind clear." Within a couple of years after the eruption, however, vegetation on Kodiak was growing more lush that before.

The next two decades draped Kodiak in

quiet obscurity. Life for the town's few hundred people revolved around herring and salmon fishing, occasional dances, and the gossip gleaned off the single telephone party line. During the summer, boats from Outside docked every few weeks, bringing everyone to the harbor for the latest news.

Then the military descended, to build a naval base as part of a larger Alaska fortification on the eve of World War II. The place buzzed with thousands of construction workers and soldiers, and new structures sprouted overnight. Some estimates put more than 20,000 people on Kodiak during the peak of military construction.

After the frantic pace of the war years ended, Kodiak settled down to the business of fishing. Salmon, herring and shellfish occupied fishermen, who delivered to several large local canneries. The military maintained its presence after the war, practically doubling Kodiak's population. A few ranchers raised cattle on government land, lauding Kodiak as a stockman's paradise while shooting bears to protect their herds. Bear-cattle conflicts influenced the creation of Kodiak National Wildlife Refuge in 1941, to protect bears and their habitat.

By the early 1960s, king crab emerged as Kodiak's new bonanza. During the height of the fishery, tons of the giant crustaceans were hauled from the region's waters and by the late 1960s, Kodiak led the nation's ports in value of product landed. As king crab stocks declined through the 1970s, Kodiak's fishermen added shrimp and other crab species to their seasonal mix of herring, salmon and halibut. The 1980s brought Americanization of the bottomfish fishery, previously dominated by the Japanese, and

many of Kodiak's fishermen refitted their boats to participate. Kodiak's port continues today as one of the most active fishing ports in the nation.

Kodiak's people are a tenacious lot, rebounding from numerous disasters in record times. In addition to the 1912 Katmai eruption of Novarupta, the Good Friday earthquake of 1964 and the 1989 *Exxon Valdez* crude oil spill in Prince William Sound were benchmark calamities.

The earthquake — the most powerful ever measured on the North American continent — and seismic sea waves that followed killed 20 people in the Kodiak region and did an estimated $45 million in property damage through the archipelago. Water swamped downtown Kodiak, wiped out three villages and crippled another. Haunting stories abound from people who barely escaped the rushing waters or watched waves batter their homes, churches, boats and businesses, ripping them from foundations and moorings and spinning them crazily into each other or out to sea. The quake dropped the ground as much as six feet in some places, lifted it in others. The fishing industry, particularly the burgeoning crab fishery, reeled from devastation. Some 225 fishing boats were lost or damaged, several canneries and cold storage facilities disappeared, and docks broke apart. Recovery was relatively swift as people regrouped and rebuilt, but those who lived through the experience still speak in terms of "before" and "after" the earthquake.

The oil spill, which unleashed nearly 11 million gallons of crude, hurt the Kodiak region emotionally and economically. Oil slimed some shores in the island group, as

currents carried it west from the wrecked Exxon Oil Co. tanker on Bligh Reef outside Valdez. The spill shut down fishing in Kodiak's coastal waters and limited subsistence activities. Many boat owners made big bucks by contracting their vessels for clean-up efforts, but serious rifts emerged between those who did and did not get contracts. Fishing resumed in 1990, and in 1992 the oil spill clean-up activities were officially ended. In the immediate aftermath, a Kodiak fishermen's support group, consisting mostly of women who called themselves "The Crude Wives" formed, and from them sprang the grassroots Kodiak Environmental Network, which is now addressing a number of issues through public forums.

It is with heightened awareness that the people of Kodiak look to the future, to the health of the ocean, its fish and the effects of human activities on their island world.

In June 1912, Novarupta volcano near Mount Katmai on the Alaska Peninsula erupted and ash rained down on Kodiak for two days, piling up 18 inches deep. This postcard shows the scene two weeks later when people were still digging out. (Courtesy of Nicki Nielsen)

Military Buildup on Kodiak

Kodiak grew into the biggest of three naval bases in Alaska during World War II. With an air station, submarine base and joint command center for the Navy, Army and Army Air Force, Kodiak became the principal advance naval base in the North Pacific. Coordinating with naval bases at Sitka to the east and Dutch Harbor to the west, Kodiak's seaplanes made vital patrols of the Gulf of Alaska, Bering Sea and North Pacific. Its ships and submarines played critical roles in the Aleutian campaign to combat the Japanese.

In the 1930s, military strategists considered the possibility of war in the Pacific and recognized Alaska's defensive position. In 1937, the Navy built a small seaplane base at Sitka, the only military installation in Alaska outside the Army's tiny Chilkoot Barracks near Haines. Late in

Fort Abercrombie at Miller Point was one of three Army subposts. Today it is a state historical park where visitors can see remains of two 8-inch gun emplacements, ammunition magazines, commander's station and other structures. (Don Pitcher)

1938, a naval board recommended expanding Sitka's base and establishing seaplane/submarine bases at Kodiak and Dutch Harbor. Kodiak's location and ample anchorages made it particularly attractive. As war escalated in Europe and Japan's activity increased in Asia, Congress approved money for widespread fortifications in Alaska. Construction began the next year on Kodiak's naval base, along with an Army base to defend it. Civilian contractor Siems Drake Puget Sound started the job, and the Naval Construction Battalions (Seabees) gradually took over.

The first Army soldiers, about 175 of them, arrived April 1941 at Kodiak's Fort Greely, named after arctic explorer Maj. Gen. Adolphus W. Greely. In July, some of the first Navy seaplanes arrived from Washington state. Bad weather in the Gulf of Alaska forced them into Kodiak just skimming the waves, guided by an uncalibrated radio station on Woody Island. As soon as the squadron leader saw rocks and spruce trees, the planes "fell out of the air like a flock of wounded ducks," according to Lt. James Russell, only to find out they

This abandoned World War II bunker on Long Island was part of the Army's Fort Tidball subpost, with a 6-inch sea coast gun battery and support facilities. (Roz Goodman)

had landed on a channel between Afognak and Kodiak islands.

The number of troops escalated quickly. By September 1941, Fort Greely had more than 3,000 men, with housing so tight that some moved into motor sheds.

Strangers swarmed the quiet island fishing

ABOVE: *The military's extensive sea coast defense included this outpost at Narrow Cape. (Charles Kay)*

TOP RIGHT: *This abandoned World War II bunker on Spruce Cape is an important landmark, with a navigation daymark and light to guide boats near town. (Marion Stirrup)*

RIGHT: *The road to Chiniak ends at Sequel Point, another World War II sea coast defense outpost. (Charles Kay)*

town, the newcomers etching Kodiak's landscape with roads, buildings, bunkers, docks, air strips and lots of gun batteries. They also brought new money, and Kodiak's small downtown jangled with the sound of change. Charles Madsen, one of Kodiak's first bear hunting guides, ran the town's only hotel and realized early on that time was ripe to offer souvenirs. He opened Totem Igloo Curio and Gift Shop stocked with parkas, mukluks and baleen, along with satin pillowcases decorated with fringe. Thelma Madsen Johnson, his daughter who was then 19 and worked at the store, recalls the shop packed with soldiers. Sometimes she would have to lock the doors because no more bodies could fit inside.

The young, uniformed men romanced the local girls, and filled their free time with picnics, hikes, movies, USO dances, skating parties and ski dates at the military's ski chalet in Anton Larsen pass. A popular outing was to Long Island by boat.

The bombing of Pearl Harbor, Dec. 7, 1941, put Kodiak and other Alaska bases on the front line. Local folks stepped up their beach patrols. Blackout conditions were imposed and the soldiers went on 24-hour alerts. Kodiak's military installations were far from complete. Only a hanger and runways had been finished on the naval base and although the Army's harbor defenses were mostly in place, the garrison had only a 17-minute supply of ammunition.

Construction crews peaked in May 1942 at nearly 3,000, as the military anticipated Japanese activity in the North Pacific, including an attack on Dutch Harbor. Rear Adm. Robert Theobald, commander of the Navy's North Pacific Force, arrived in Kodiak in late May aboard his flagship USS *Nashville*. The atmosphere, according to a squadron diarist Lt. Billy Wheeler, was "tense, expectant and hurried...."

The Army's defenses included gun batteries, searchlight, fire control and radar installations around the northeast coast of Kodiak Island, with outposts on Long, Puffin and Spruce islands. The Harbor Defense Fire Control Communications System linked 57 locations with hundreds of thousands of feet of underwater and underground communications cable. In addition, long-range aircraft warning radars were located at Cape Chiniak on northeast Kodiak Island and at Lazy Bay on the southeast side of the island; Cape Chiniak's radar was one of two in Alaska's coastal network operating when the Japanese bombed Dutch Harbor on June 3, 1942.

As the Aleutian campaign intensified, Kodiak became joint command headquarters for the Navy and the Eleventh Air Force. The Royal Canadian Air Force stationed planes at Kodiak, too.

In April 1943, the Army opened three subposts: Fort Tidball on Long Island; Fort J.H. Smith at Cape Chiniak; and Fort Abercrombie at Miller Point. The Army reached full strength December 1943 with 11,000 men. Some estimates put the total number of military and civilian personnel during the height of the buildup on Kodiak at 20,000. From February 1943 to June 1944, 192 ocean-going vessels discharged or loaded more than 183,000 mean tons of cargo at the Army's 900-foot dock, an expansion of Otto Kraft's original dock.

Troops began leaving the island in 1944, and the Army post was put in caretaking status. The former Navy and Army installations are now one reservation administered by the U.S. Coast Guard. Many of the naval structures are still used by the Coast Guard, but few Army structures remain. The military runways are leased by commercial and private air companies. The two large seaplane hangers at the head of Womens Bay have been updated by $10 million, and serve Coast Guard planes and helicopters. Coast Guard family housing occupies part of the old Fort Greely site. The Buskin State Recreation Park encompasses the Buskin Hill outpost, which still has two 155mm Panama gun mounts. Remains of the underground Harbor Defense Command Post on Artillery Hill are still visible. Fort Abercrombie, at Miller Point, today is a state historical park.

BELOW: *The quiet fishing village of Kodiak was never quite the same after the military and its band arrived. (Courtesy of Michael Nore)*

RIGHT: *Lena Boeckman, right, and Catherine Blankenberg obliged to pose with three Navy men in Kodiak in 1942. "Wished to send snaps to wives to show them they were not lonely with 2 gran'mas near," noted Ms. Boeckman on the back of the picture. (Courtesy of Michael Nore)*

Tom Shugak, Uncle Principal

BY TOM SHUGAK

I was born in Old Harbor on October 24, 1941. The name on my birth certificate was Thomas Bill Shugak, Jr. Later I found out I was not a junior, so I wrote the Bureau of Vital Statistics to drop the junior. My parents, Willie and Flora Shugak, were originally from Eagle Harbor in Kiluda Bay.

My earliest recollections of Old Harbor are few. I seem to have a mental block about them. I remember playing boats with Carl Christiansen. Fathers and uncles made the boats, each with a miniature hold that we would fill with miniature salmon caught at high tide with miniature seines in the lagoon's grasses. I am glad there were not too many boys in this small community; we would have killed off the salmon runs.

Dad talked about the whaling station at Port Hobron, five miles northeast of Old

A fishing boat cruises Kodiak waters near Old Harbor. Fishing remains the mainstay of commerce in the area. (D. Menke)

Harbor. The company employed some young men of the village. The men would row back and forth to the village when they had free time. Burning blubber could be smelled in Old Harbor when a northerly would blow.

The herring fishery was healthy. A saltery was built on the shores of Old Harbor and across the straits in Port Otto.

The men commercial fished in the summers. The Seven Rivers area south of Old Harbor was a hot spot. Tenders towed large skiffs to the area, and the men camped on the beach. When the tender returned at high tide, one skiff skipper set his siwash seine (hand purse) and the others held the corks. One set filled the tender. Crews camped until the next tide. The style of boats changed every few years. When larger vessels were available, some fishermen worked the Red River area on the west side of Kodiak Island. The end-of-season payoff was not large by current standards; $300 bought a winter's supply of grub, .22-gauge shotgun shells were a quarter for 50 rounds.

Subsistence played a large part then as it does today in the lives of Native people. Spring brings halibut which is usually eaten

Tom Shugak is the first Native from Old Harbor to work in the school there as a certified teacher. (Courtesy of Tom Shugak)

fresh, but sometimes dried. Herring are used for pickling or bait. Red salmon come next and are eaten fresh or smoked. Most of the red salmon are caught in Moser and Olga bays by friends in Akhiok, or by late herring fishermen waiting for Alaska Department of Fish and Game openings. Pink and chum salmon are dried in the cool, dry fall and eaten fresh in summer and fall. Silver salmon are salted, smoked and frozen. Some residents catch silvers from November through January, when they are best dried. Shellfish are gathered year-round, but mainly in winter. Berries are picked in season.

During the 1930s, '40s and '50s, tuberculosis was one of the diseases that devastated the Alutiiq people. Sanatoriums were built in Juneau, Seward, Anchorage and Mount Edgecumbe. My mother was sent to a hospital in Juneau in 1946 and died there in 1947. My father was in and out of the hospital in Anchorage with the disease. Both of my sisters, Jennie Ann and Mabel, and I tested positive for TB at an early age. Twin sisters died of influenza in the 1940s.

My father, Willie, a commercial fisherman and trapper, was unable to care for us by himself. Grandfather Innokenti helped with my two sisters. I was sent to the Kodiak Baptist Mission in 1947. The mission was originally on Woody Island, but the main buildings burned in 1936 and the mission was rebuilt two miles north of Kodiak. Another mission building was built at Ouzinkie. The white-and-green, two-story mission buildings housed 15 to 20 children each from six Kodiak area villages: Ouzinkie, Afognak, Larsen Bay, Karluk, Akhiok and Old Harbor. Children also came from southcentral Alaska, the Alaska Peninsula and Aleutian chain.

I remember leaving Old Harbor one sunny day on a Seabee, a two-passenger amphibious airplane, with a Russian Orthodox priest as my chaperon. Our first stop was at Shearwater Cannery in Kiluda Bay.

That spring was the first time I had not gone to Shearwater with my family. Families were taken on a Kadiak Fisheries salmon tender every spring to prepare the cannery for the salmon season. The tender towed the workers' skiffs. Families rode in the open, canvas-covered fish deck. I knew when it was time to go by gauging the growth of the horsetails. Once they appeared, it was time to begin looking for the barge.

I do not remember much of my first airplane ride. Grandfather Innokenti and Dad met me in Shearwater and gave me a tearful goodbye. My father had learned the seine-mending and -making business there and was web boss for many years.

William Stone, new superintendent of the mission, picked me up in Kodiak. Mr. Stone broke the ice by stopping at Montmarte Inn for my first ice cream cone. It was sure good. I threw the cone out the window because I did not know what to do with it.

The next morning I sat with 15 other children at two connected tables and, after grace, I watched what each did with a round orange thing on their plates. Then I ate my first orange.

I was afraid and homesick for a long time at the mission. The English language was difficult. Vera Lukavitch (Marvin) helped me adjust by interpreting. A year later I sang a solo at the Baptist Church.

My education had started at Old Harbor. I spent two years in kindergarten, entering in August one year and in October the next. This was not unusual. Old Bureau of Indian Affairs progress reports show that some students were kept in some grades for two or three years. Dad was kicked out of school in the fifth grade and told to go trapping. He trapped with his dad at Ugak Bay, and continued on his own at Kiluda and Boulder bays and at Gull Cape Lagoon. Dad would take us when he could, so the date of our first day of school was determined by when we would return from fishing or trapping.

Our house parents at the mission tried to get us ready for the outside world by demanding excellence in school and in our chores. Ms. Green, my house parent for many years, gave me Chet Atkins records if I made the honor roll. Mrs. Fields gave me piano lessons until baseball got the best of me. The men gave us practical experience. The boys built barns and garages, dug ditches, painted, pulled nails from salvaged boards, gardened, caught red and silver salmon for winter food, cut hay, branded cattle and butchered. I worked in Dr. A. Holmes Johnson's garden for several summers and was janitor at the Kodiak Baptist Church.

I graduated on May 25, 1960. Many of us from the mission were lost and confused not long after we left. We were mission kids, not belonging with our parents and not belonging at the mission. My first scholarship offer was from Alaska Methodist (now Pacific) University. I was leery of going because my friends Milton Souter, now a judge, Billy Fern, a teacher, and Norman Saxton, an accountant, also received scholarships. They were sharp. It took me longer to complete lessons. I opted to go to the smaller Sheldon Jackson Junior College in Sitka.

Sheldon Jackson was also safe. It was similar to what I had just left. Basketball kept me in high school and did the same for me in college. The choir I joined traveled to Ketchikan, Angoon and Hoonah. I graduated with an Associate of Arts degree and married soon after.

1964 brought the earthquake and resulting tsunami that destroyed Old Harbor, Afognak village, Kaguyak and low-lying areas of Kodiak and Ouzinkie. Alaska Department of Fish and Game had taken me on in early March to help with Kodiak Island's salmon stream survey. Our crew had gotten into Kodiak on the research and patrol vessel *Kittywake* in the early afternoon of March 27th after surveying many

streams. A shower, and the steaks we badly needed after weeks of Starlite food, were our greatest worries. Then the earthquake hit. We ran outside.

There was a loud rumbling coming from the north. The Kodiak slide area to the south was so dusty we could not see the road. We were walking on jelly. The electrical lines were swaying dangerously. It was sobering to realize how fragile human beings are on this powerful earth. We jumped on a truck and headed for high ground as directed by the police.

TOP RIGHT: *Although offered a scholarship to Alaska Pacific (then Alaska Methodist) University, Tom chose to attend Sheldon Jackson Junior College in Sitka after he graduated from high school in 1960. (Tom Shugak)*

LOWER RIGHT: *In 1981 Tom Shugak graduated from Alaska Pacific University with an elementary teaching certificate and was assigned a class at Old Harbor, where he lived as a youngster. This photo shows the old school at the primarily Native community on the southeast coast of Kodiak Island. (Tom Shugak)*

Several hundred people watched and listened as the tsunamis came. High combers swept Long and Woody islands' reefs. By the time the waves reached the city they were babies, but what devastation they brought. No more than super tides, the three waves pushed the town inland several blocks. The captain of the tender *Selief* called in. The dispatcher, Mrs. Peggy Dyson, asked him where he was and listened in disbelief as he pinpointed his location. The tender was behind the school, three blocks inland.

Noise from the destruction continued throughout the night. Many homeless tried

Tom Shugak's father, Willie, mended and made seine nets at Shearwater Cannery for years. In 1926 Kadiak Fisheries built the cannery to take advantage of strong pink salmon runs on the east side of Kodiak Island. The cannery closed about 1958 and was destroyed in the 1964 earthquake. (Violet Able, courtesy of Tom Shugak)

to sleep at the high school, now the Kodiak Junior High building. The morning brought sadness. Downtown was gone. Looting was taking place. Alaska Department of Fish and Game personnel were at that time deputized to enforce certain fishing laws. Badges were handed out when personnel were hired. Our survey crew, given more power because of the emergency, assisted police in patrol of the downtown area. The city fathers rebounded quickly. The National Guard and other military maintained peace. Canned goods were taken to the National Guard Armory and disinfected by townspeople. There were many potlucks at the school. The volunteer chefs had no way to tell what they were opening because the labels had been washed off.

After the quake, the residents of Old Harbor, Kaguyak and Afognak were eventually taken to Anchorage, where they stayed the winter. Families returned to Old Harbor in spring 1965 to begin rebuilding. Kaguyak residents were scattered, some moving to Akhiok, some to Old Harbor and others to Kodiak. The village was never rebuilt. Afognak villagers moved to Kizuyak Bay, naming their new village Port Lions.

After my job with the salmon stream surveys was finished, we moved to Juneau to look for work. The Alaska Department of Fish and Game Protection Division needed help, and my first job was to clean outboard motors that survived the tsunami in Kodiak. Later I enrolled at Fort Lewis College in Durango, Colo.

In 1975 I dropped out of school and moved back to Old Harbor. The community had changed; the tsunami had had its effect. The people did not seem the same. My

uncle's store was gone. The old herring saltery we used to play in was gone. The missionary, Violet Able, had moved to Anchorage. My grandfather, the lay reader in the Russian Orthodox Church, had died immediately after moving back from Anchorage. The fish processor *Sonya* had come, giving people steady work. King crab were at their peak. The community had grown. With the help of government agencies, a boat harbor had been built. When I was in Old Harbor last, we had to row to the boats anchored in front of the village. Before and during storms, men and young boys would help each other pull large skiffs up the beach, singing our traditional working song, pulling in unison to each command. Nobody had to do that anymore. Before the tsunami, every household had to get a winter's supply of fuel from the cannery tender and roll the 55-gallon oil drums from the beach to their homes. Everybody helped each other. Now there was a pump truck. Before groceries were purchased in large lots from Columbia Wards Fisheries tenders and had to be skiffed to shore. Now there were two grocery stores.

I lived in Old Harbor and Kodiak for several years, commercial salmon fishing in summers and working various jobs in the winter. One place I always seemed to gravitate to was the school. I began my school career as the dayman, doing whatever was demanded. The next winter was my first experience in the classroom, as a teacher's aide at Old Harbor. One year the school district needed a teacher. I taught health, physical education, biology, outboard motor repair, outdoor survival and elementary mathematics with an emergency certificate for $10,000 per year. I still have a copy of that contract. I earned more as an aide.

In 1977-1978, my wife, Fran, and I talked about school. Alaska Pacific University accepted all of my previously earned credits, so we moved to Anchorage with $3,000; three school-age girls, Ardith, Susan and Marcia; and a baby, December. An older son Charley and a daughter Terrilyn worked in Kodiak. Two boys, William and Alex, stayed with their natural mother in Old Harbor. Terese was in Juneau. Twenty-one-year-old Jimmy lived in Anchorage and died shortly after we were settled. Fran worked two jobs to get me through school and support the family. In 1981 I graduated with an elementary teaching certificate.

The Kodiak Island Borough School District had an opening at Old Harbor. The Kodiak Area Native Association helped, without my knowledge, in securing that position. My first year was different from any of the jobs I had had before. The gold-fish-bowl syndrome fits my situation well. I was the first Native from Old Harbor to graduate and work in the school as a certificated teacher. It seemed that everybody was watching, the community, my family, teachers, the principal, and most of all the central office. Many mornings 4:30 came too early as I prepared for class. After the first teachers' meeting, I went to the Old Harbor Post Office for mail. The postmaster asked me if I was allowed into the teachers' meetings.

After six years at Old Harbor School we needed a change. The only schools I had experienced were Old Harbor and Mountain View School in Anchorage where I student taught. I was offered and accepted a fifth-grade class at East School in Kodiak. What a

change. The children, parents, teachers and principal were all helpful, but the number of children increased from the multigrade classroom of 17 to 19 in Old Harbor to nearly 30 busy fifth-graders in Kodiak. The next year I asked for the fourth grade in the same school. The numbers were less, and the children still loved their teachers at that age.

The school district's assistant superintendent had talked to me about working on my master's degree because I was interested in curriculum development. I explored Sabbatical leave. The school board accepted my application in March 1990, and Fran, December and I left for the University of Alaska Fairbanks that fall after salmon fishing in Bristol Bay.

Our year went quickly. In May, the Kodiak Island Borough School District superintendent, John Witteveen, offered me the principal's position at Old Harbor. Word of my appointment had spread by the time we arrived in August. Many people were happy for us; others were skeptical. The children could not believe I was their principal. I am related to so many that some call me "Uncle Principal."

The town has changed in the three years we have been gone. The residents control how our community is to grow. Outside agencies approach the community in a different way, giving people credit for intelligence and knowledge on how to handle

certain problems. Tourism and guided hunting and fishing has begun, but in a small way to avoid greatly impacting the subsistence lifestyle. A lodge and restaurant serve the community and visitors. The tribal and city councils are becoming viable organizations. The Old Harbor Native Corp. is exploring ways to increase profits for shareholders. The new airfield funded this year by the legislature will be longer. The new school and newly renovated gymnasium are valued by students, parents and other community members. The city council is exploring the feasibility of a hydroelectric plant. The tiny, sleepy village is no more.

John Gibbons, Kodiak Cowboy

BY D. SUTHERLAND FOLLOWS

Editor's note: *D. Sutherland Follows is a former National Park Service employee and now a free-lance writer and photographer who specializes in interpretation of Alaska's natural and cultural features. He currently is Tourism Director for the Resource Development Council for Alaska.*

On a warm spring day in 1941 the steamship *Yukon* steered toward the Kodiak docks to complete another long passage from Seattle. Standing on deck was a tall cowboy from southcentral Idaho named John A. Gibbons.

John had been born February 9, 1912, the seventh of nine children in an Irish immigrant family. His father had worked the silver mines south of Ketchum, Idaho,

Remains of the Port Hobron whaling station on Sitkalidak Island's north shore lie rusting in the tundra. John Gibbons spent several happy years working on a cattle and horse ranch on the island near Old Harbor. (Chlaus Lotscher)

in what is now the Sun Valley area. In 1883, John's father homesteaded 160 acres on the Camas Prairie, not far from Old Soldier, Idaho, and began raising horses and cattle.

The *Yukon*'s horn loudly blasted a signal to the distant shore. Land ahead. John looked out across calm seas toward verdant islands. It was an unusually sunny day for Kodiak Island, but nothing like the high desert sun John was leaving behind him. Little did he realize then that Alaska would be his home for more than half a century.

Gibbons had hired on as a civilian carpenter to build the Kodiak Naval Station. His bride, Margaret Lightfoot Lee, remained in Washington until John could find a place for her. Margie was an accomplished singer, dancer and actress who had appeared on Broadway and worked in Mack Sennett Productions in Hollywood. When their trails crossed in Hollywood, John and Margie fell in love.

John had been lured to Hollywood because of his good fortunes at Sun Valley, where he had met Samuel Goldwyn and others connected with the movie industry. William Averell Harriman, son of the Union

Pacific Railroad magnate Edward Henry Harriman, developed Sun Valley Lodge and Resort, where John won the horse concession contract.

Hollywood was no place for John Gibbons. He found some work there supplying horses for western movies and doing stunt work. Sometimes he would stand in for western star Randolph Scott or for Jimmy Stewart. Any tall, trim actor who needed a stand-in served John's needs as well as theirs. John always kept good horses, that was his trade. John prided himself on being a darn good horseman.

During the Great Depression, a person did whatever they could to get work. The only cash around was at rodeos where John tried his hand at everything. He rode bucking broncs and clung to the shifting hides of Brahman bulls. He bulldogged steers and roped calves so large "they'd be looking you in the eye when you got off to throw them." A few dollars and a few bones down the line, John found his calling as a proficient calf roper. Even at that, there never was enough money for him in the rodeo business.

Looking back on his wilder days at Sun

John A. Gibbons, holding the Alaska flag, sits astride his favorite white gelding, Old Joe. The horse, with John aboard, often pranced down the main street of Kodiak during the annual Fourth of July parade. (Courtesy of D. Sutherland Follows)

Valley, John takes it all in stride. To win the horse concession, he had invested in good stock horses, sleighs, new tack, feed and all the incidentals. It was risky, but John hoped his services would be in demand by the invited guests, skiers, European nobility, Hollywood moguls, stars and assorted freeloaders who would show up for the gala opening of the resort on December 20, 1936.

Developer Averell Harriman had long dreamed of finding the ideal location with perfect snow for his resort. Sun Valley won. It just happened to be at the end of his railroad line in Ketchum, less than a mile from his planned development.

In early December 1936, however, Sun Valley was hurting. Only a scoff of snow had fallen. The runners on John's horse sleighs flashed sparks all the way from the train depot to the new lodge. Everyone was worried, especially John who had everything tied up in this venture. The grand opening was held anyway.

The next day, the steel-gray skies burst open like a ruptured featherbed. Large, white flakes floated down, depositing nearly 2 feet of powder snow. John's horse-drawn sleighs did a bustling business, and those he rigged for skijoring proved just as popular. To celebrate, some of the Sun Valley boys went into Ketchum to see what was happening at the old Casino Bar. The owner had earlier arranged for John to encourage the lodge crowd to visit his place in town. John was to ride in on his horse and fire a shot from his Colt revolver. The photographers who had covered the lodge opening were already in the bar when John arrived with his horse Old Slim. Among the photographers was *Life* magazine's Alfred Eisenstadt. On the boardwalk outside the bar and totally unaware of the plot was Hungarian actress Rene Kiss. When she saw John approaching on Old Slim, she purred, "How about a ride, cowboy?" John spurred Old Slim onto the boardwalk and swept Ms. Kiss onto the back of his horse. Horse, rider and actress made their grand entrance.

The event was not without mishap. As John moved Old Slim through the door and into the large gambling hall, he drew his gun and fired a shot into the ceiling. Old Slim lunged forward, John bumped his head on the overhead log beam, and Rene dismounted. A few minutes later, an angry, half-shaven man with his suspenders hanging from his pants showed up to complain to the bartender. He had been using the bedroom upstairs over the bar. "That crazed cowpoke could have killed me," he snarled. "Bad timing the way I see it," countered the bartender, wiping up some spilled suds. It seems the man was shaving over the washstand when the slug ripped through the floor and nearly took the straight razor right out of his hand.

John chuckles at the memory, and at how Averell Harriman had once suggested that John try his luck in Alaska. Young Averell had been aboard the *George W. Elder*, when his father chartered the steamship for the Harriman Expedition of 1899 along Alaska's coast. Averell Harriman thought there would be good opportunities for an enterprising young man who wanted to head north to see the country. John's uncle had even done as much as a gold prospector in the Klondike and at Nome.

The *Yukon* shuddered, and John came back to reality. Black smoke belched from the center stack of the *Yukon* as she adjusted her course and decreased speed. John could now see the dock where a crowd from town was gathering to survey the latest cheechakos. The ship's gangway was lowered as soon as the steamer sided into the dock and tied down onto the bollards. John lifted his duffel and joined the long line of disembarking men down the narrow gangway. Halfway down, rough voices rang out from the crowd on the dock, "There's John Gibbons. Looks like he's been rode hard and put away wet." They all laughed.

John smiled as he recognized the ringleader. "Why if it isn't old Jack McCord," John shouted. "And here I thought I was leaving all the outlaws back in Idaho." The crowd roared. John had met McCord in Nevada before coming to Alaska.

Jack McCord had made a name for himself as a gold prospector and miner. He had left the creeks of Iditarod when the town went bust about 1907. The author of Alaska's first grazing lease law, McCord had predicted that the Kodiak region would one day become famous for its cattle and sheep grazing. Jack and John would later become involved in livestock ventures.

Things were busy in Kodiak, and John's work went well. By fall, he had a place for Margie, who came up on the six-day passage aboard the SS *Denali*.

With the outbreak of World War II only two months after Margie arrived from Washington, John found his civilian job frozen as part of the war effort. John wanted to enlist and wear the Army uniform as his brothers had done, but the military found his skills too diverse to let him change jobs. The Army was preparing for a major war with the Japanese, and John progressed through civilian ranks to positions of high authority as he traveled throughout the state supervising construction projects, including White Alice communication sites and the road that snakes off Pillar Mountain on Kodiak.

When the war ended, Wakefield Fisheries picked up John as an engineer to supervise the revamping of the herring reduction plant on Raspberry Island. The company was converting their operation to the processing of king crab.

John the horseman continued to practice the skills of his cowboy culture. He produced the first rodeo in 1951 at the Tom Nelson Ranch at Kalsin Bay. His horse races were a regular Fourth of July event on the main street in Kodiak until they wiped out some of the onlookers. One of the racing horses drifted off line and ran into the crowd, hurting several people seriously. One fellow who had his face slammed into the gravel ended up with bluish marks on his forehead from embedded debris. First aid was lacking at the scene because both town doctors had been hit by the horse. The bluish marks might not have been so bad except that they created some attention from strangers. The marks spelled "I.O.U." "You didn't know whether to smile or cry, but you'd better not do neither," John remarked.

In a promotion stunt for the Casino Bar in Ketchum, Idaho, a young John A. Gibbons leads his horse, Old Slim, into the bar with Hungarian actress Rene Kiss riding behind. As part of the stunt, John fired a shot from his revolver into the ceiling, much to the disgust of a tenant in the room above who was trying to shave. (Courtesy of D. Sutherland Follows)

Eight Stars of Gold On A Field Of Blue

PHOTO COURTESY OF D. SUTHERLAND FOLLOWS

John Ben Benson, Jr., better known as Benny, was born at Chignik on the Alaska Peninsula, October 12, 1913. His mother, Tatiana, died when Benny was a toddler; and his father, John Ben Benson, a Swedish fisherman, sent Ben and his younger brother, Carl, to the Jesse Lee Home at Unalaska in the Aleutians. The Methodists operated the Jesse Lee Home as a boarding facility for children. In 1925, the home was relocated to Seward on Resurrection Bay in southcentral Alaska, and Benny and Carl went with it.

The same year, George A. Parks, governor of the Territory of Alaska, realized that Alaska did not have a territorial flag. He mentioned the lack to an official of the American Legion, who passed the word to their patriotism committee. The Legion organized a contest for all Alaska schoolchildren, grades 7 through 12, for the 1926-27 school year. A committee of senators and representatives from the Territory of Alaska and three judges selected by the American Legion chose Benny Benson's design of eight stars in the shape of the Big Dipper and North Star on a field of dark blue as the winning design.

Benny stayed with the Jesse Lee Home through his graduation from Seward High School, then returned to Chignik and to Chirikof Island in the Kodiak archipelago to help his father fur farm. He later married a Seattle resident, Betty Van Hise, and lived with her and their two daughters in various Seattle suburbs. Many summers he returned to Alaska to fish, working for several years on the fishing boats of Capt. Harry W. Crosby, grandfather of singer Bing Crosby.

Finally Benny and his daughters returned to Kodiak to live, and where he became friends with John Gibbons. Benny worked as an airplane mechanic, and represented Alaska at functions nationwide. He remarried in 1971 to Anna Sophie Jenks, who had also been raised at the Jesse Lee Home. Then on July 2, 1972, Benny died of a heart attack at Kodiak.

The annual Fourth of July parade would consistently see John on his favorite horse, Old Joe. With John carrying a massive Alaska territorial flag, the cowboy and Old Joe made many proud trips down main street in Kodiak.

Old Joe was among the most famous horses that ever lived on Kodiak Island. He was practically the town mascot. A tall, white gelding with a pink nose, Old Joe loved children. He had patience with children, allowing them to crawl over and under him and ride bareback four at a time. But John was the only adult that had better try to ride Old Joe. The pair always had kids trailing after them. John taught many of them to rope and tie knots. Little cowboys would emerge each summer and rope fence posts and stray dogs.

When former Kodiak resident Neil Pestrakoff was 8, John taught him to rope. Tired of fence posts and sisters, Neil threw a loop as his mother came by on her bicycle. Perfect shot, but the rope caught her around the neck and jerked her off the metal mount. "I almost hung my own mother," the man laments, looking back. "And she never let me forget it either," Neil remembers.

When town officials removed the hitching posts and rails from Kodiak's main street, John had no place to tie up Old Joe. When he tried using the new parking meters, the town sheriff was not happy. He even wanted Joe to stand 10 feet back from the walkway to avoid being a health hazard.

That left little choice for John and Joe. From then on, John rode Joe into the bar where the horse ate ham sandwiches and washed them down with beer. The locals loved it. Only once did Old Joe leave a happy accident inside the bar. That occurred when some blurry-eyed fisherman took a kick at Joe's rump as he and John were going out the front door. "Joe was quick to leave a parting tribute on that feller's gum boot," chuckles John. The town mourned when Joe was found dead at the base of a sea cliff one day.

John kept his hand in ranching and the raising of fine horses by his association with a homestead on Sitkalidak Island that Jack McCord had owned at one time. The place had acres of grass belly-high to a horse. The owners hired John for several years to oversee the ranch, which consisted of 500 head of cattle and about 60 horses. John built line camps to keep men and horses out of the wind and rain that raged across the island. John loved that place and the horses he raised there.

John does not like to talk about what happened to the land, horses and cattle because it brings him much sadness. The grazing lands leased from the Bureau of Land Management were included in the land selections under the Alaska Native Claims Settlement Act of 1971. With no place to move the livestock, the ranch owners lost everything.

John and Margie moved to Anchorage, where they continued to be active in civic affairs. Margie died a couple of years ago and is buried in Kodiak.

John A. Gibbons presents a portrait of Benny Benson to Ms. Barbara Garrison, principal of the Benson Secondary School in Anchorage during the school's first graduation ceremony in May 1992. (D. Sutherland Follows)

As an active octogenarian, John Gibbons continues his many interests in Alaska affairs, especially the promotion of pioneer activities. He still loves fine horses, Alaska history and travel. He contributes time to those who want to learn horseman skills, especially the tying of knots and splices. These meant security for men and equipment, and to watch John tie a turks head, fedor and Spanish rose is a testimony to necessity and skill.

John the horseman has a philosophy about giving everyone a fair shot to prove their worth. "It isn't always the thoroughbred that reaches the mark in the greater race of life. It is often that crossbred, nonconformed stock horse whose clear vision, stamina and untamed spirit exceeds all expectations."

Making A Living

To know something of Kodiak's heartbeat, take a walk down by the docks and past the canneries along the waterfront. Watch the boats, smell the air, hear the talk. Kodiak is fishing, and evidence abounds.

Some 800 locally owned fishing boats homeport in Kodiak's St. Paul harbor and it is frequented by another 4,500 vessels a year. Nearly 120 of the boats based here are 80 feet or longer, making it the state's largest commercial fishing port and the hub for the western Alaska fishery. Kodiak's port consistently ranks in the nation's top three in volume and value. Something is always going on. Corky McCorkle, harbormaster for the past 21 years, monitors the comings and goings from huge windows that line the wall of his second-story office. "I've seen it all. I've watched the industry grow from a sleepy summer salmon fishery to a multimillion-dollar year-round industry," he says. In 1992, a $32 million harbor expansion project got underway after three decades of dreams and planning. The expansion includes the new St. Herman breakwater and about 178 additional boat slips, most of which will be for 90-foot and larger commercial fishing vessels. When completed sometime in 1996, the new St. Herman harbor at 90 acres, with the existing St. Paul harbor will make the largest protected commercial fishing harbor in the United States, McCorkle says.

It is hard to precisely define what Kodiak's fishing industry means to the community. But without salmon, pollock, cod, crab, halibut and the other types of seafood brought to shore, Kodiak would not exist as it is today. In 1992, area residents held more than 2,100 commercial fishing permits. About 1,400 worked harvesting fish, as boat captains and crew members earning nearly $102 million, the 1991 ex-vessel value of seafood landed in Kodiak. In addition to the fishing boats homeported here, some 120 more are based in the six villages, for which Kodiak is the service center. During 1991,

Seiners and a spotter plane await a herring opening at Olga Bay. Kodiak's herring sac-roe fishery has done well in recent years, with more than 4,000 tons harvested in 1992, the largest on record. (Don Pitcher)

Millie Gray, a fish and wildlife technician for the Alaska Department of Fish and Game, counts sockeye salmon as they pass through a weir from Olga Bay into South Olga Lakes. (Don Pitcher)

LEFT: *Halibut are headed to one of Kodiak's many canneries. This species accounts for Kodiak's third most valuable fishery. (Jim Simmen)*

ABOVE: *Neatly stored longlines await halibut fisherman who must bring in their catch during a series of short openings. (Jim Simmen)*

Kodiak's dozen fish processing plants employed nearly 2,000 and had a combined payroll of more than $35 million.

Kodiak's spinoffs from fishing are countless. There are fishing support businesses — marine equipment repairing and supply services, flying services that specialize in at-sea crew changes, divers who do underwater welding and hull surveys, expeditors to handle shore-side business affairs. Federal and state government agencies — the National Marine Fisheries

Service, the National Oceanic and Atmospheric Administration, and several divisions of the Alaska Department of Fish and Game — operate in Kodiak largely because of the fishing industry. Even the U.S. Coast Guard is here mostly because of Kodiak's central role in northern seas fishing. Signs of life at sea are everywhere: men and women in knee-high rubber boots; yards stacked with nets, floats and crab pots; even an odoriferous greeting from the Bio-Dry fish waste reduction plant on the highway west of town.

There are ways other than commercial fishing to make a living in the Kodiak islands, of course. The retail, business and local government sides of Kodiak resemble

those in towns of comparable size. And the resources of the archipelago feed a few other industries — logging, a little cattle ranching, sport hunting and fishing, and an increasing amount of tourism. In the past, some fur farming, whaling, ice harvesting and gold mining took place and the future may include offshore oil drilling in Shelikof Strait. An offshore lease sale is proposed here for 1994. Two previous lease sales in the region, in 1977 and 1981, resulted in some exploratory drilling but all the wells were eventually plugged and abandoned. But Kodiak is mostly hooked on commercial fishing.

The region's first people lived close to the water, hunting sea mammals and birds, fishing the island's salmon rivers, gathering beach foods and filling the gaps with land animals, berries and edible plants. The Russians came initially for sea otters. They dried and salted salmon for food, mostly taken from the Karluk River's vast runs, but their attempts at selling barrels of salted salmon were not profitable.

United States purchase of Alaska triggered development of Kodiak's salmon fishery. Salmon has been Kodiak's mainstay most of the time since then, even with its ups and downs in value and abundance. Five species are fished from Kodiak waters. Salmon consistently ranks at the top in value for fish landed; in 1991 the ex-vessel value of salmon harvested in the Kodiak region was nearly $31.5 million. In 1992, exceptional sockeye runs combined with good prices to offset an unusually poor year for pinks.

Red king crab took the spotlight during much of the 1960s and 1970s — when the salmon fishery was rebuilding from previous years of overfishing. By the time crab stocks crashed and the red king crab fishery for Kodiak ended in 1983, the salmon fishery was revitalized. The worst year recently for salmon fishermen was 1989, when the *Exxon Valdez* oil spill in Prince William Sound closed most fisheries. Kodiak's purse seine fleet and the setnetters along the island's west side were unable to fish because of oil contamination. The only commercial harvest of salmon came from a few setnetters in the Moser-Olga Bay system and from a short September opening for sockeye in Karluk Lagoon.

During the late 1980s, the groundfish fishery for pollock and cod emerged, and in 1991 groundfish ranked first in value, at nearly $34 million, of all fish landed at Kodiak. Halibut is Kodiak's third most valuable fishery with Tanner crab fourth. Other fisheries include herring, scallop, sea urchin, shrimp, Dungeness crab, brown king crab and octopus.

Groundfish are stabilizing an otherwise seasonal processing industry: salmon four months in summer, short halibut openings, winter crabbing, spring herring fishing. Pollock and cod are landed year-round and in 1992, Kodiak's shore-based processors were promised a steady supply of Gulf of Alaska groundfish, at least through 1994, by a federal fisheries management council.

Patricia Roppel details the intriguing history of Kodiak's salmon industry in her book *Salmon from Kodiak* (1986). In brief, the salmon industry in Kodiak started in 1882 with the Alaska Commercial Co.'s first cannery at Karluk Spit, at the mouth of the Karluk River. By 1889, four more canneries were operating here. During the early years when the runs of red salmon were phenomenal, Karluk Spit was the busiest fishing place in Alaska.

Canneries popped up at Larsen, Olga, Moser and Afognak bays. From 1887 to 1890, so many new canneries opened in Alaska that the amount of canned salmon quadrupled, glutting the market. Prices dived. Companies consolidated. By 1893, the Alaska Packers Association, the largest salmon canning company in the territory, controlled most of Kodiak's canneries. During this time, some salting of salmon, cod and herring was occurring in remote bays, including Ugak and Uganik, and at Port Hobron on Sitkalidak Island.

Competition flourished between canneries in the early 1900s and intense rivalries erupted. Indiscriminate fishing by the canneries, including widespread use of fish traps, resulted in large declines in red salmon. Regulations to protect salmon were enacted as early as 1896, although enforcement was a joke with only two agents assigned to all of Alaska.

Efforts to bolster salmon populations

TOP RIGHT: *Once a major fishery for Kodiak in the 1960s, the shrimp trawl fishery has been closed since 1985. Exploratory shrimp fishing is still open, however, and some boats go after spot shrimp with pots. (Steve McCutcheon)*

RIGHT: *When technology in the 1950s improved freezing capabilities, Kodiak's fisheries expanded into red king crab (male, left, and female shown here). By the 1960s, king crab brought millions of dollars to Kodiak fishermen. But the boom ended, and the fishery was closed for Kodiak in 1983. (Steve McCutcheon)*

came early. The first hatchery in 1891 was short-lived. Alaska Packers built a Karluk River hatchery in 1896, but an adjacent brackish lagoon offered poor fry habitat and though the operation lasted 21 years, its success was dubious. In 1892, the government set aside Afognak Island, Sea Lion Rocks and Sea Otter Island as the Afognak Forest and Fish Culture Reserve, the first national forest preserve in Alaska. All fishing was halted in the reserve until 1909 when it was reopened to Natives. A hatchery built in 1907 on Afognak Lake operated until 1933, when it was closed and turned over to the U.S. Navy as a recreation center.

During World War II, the Navy drafted about 25 Kodiak fishing boats to patrol. The movements of boats were restricted, as was radio contact with the canneries. Obtaining permits and transportation from the west coast for cannery workers posed logistical problems, but by 1943 the salmon industry was listed as an essential war industry.

For all its appearances before and after the war as a quiet burg, Kodiak stirred with the politics of fishing. In the beginning, the canneries imported crews of Chinese laborers from San Francisco, gradually substituting Scandinavians, Germans, Italians and Filipinos. Fishermen worked for the canneries, getting gear, supplies and even loans from the companies. In the late 1930s, labor unions started representing the workers, and unions to represent fishermen were not far behind. The fight to abolish fish traps in the territory pitted canneries against fishermen. Kodiak fishermen had to fight for a place in their own waters as the number of outside boats increased; of the 1,619 registered fishermen in Kodiak in 1950, 680 were nonresidents. This pressure brought about more stringent regulations and increased enforcement to protect the fishery.

Revitalization of the salmon fisheries in the 1960s initiated pioneering efforts, such as planting salmon eggs in barren lakes and construction of fish passes over natural barriers to help fish reach spawning grounds. Runs in the Pauls Lake system on northeast Afognak were enhanced with fish passes, and new runs that continue today were stocked in Fraser Lake, on south Kodiak Island near Olga Bay. In 1954, the government-funded Kitoi Bay Research Station on Afognak was opened to study salmon; today it is one of the larger production hatcheries in the state. It is also one of two hatcheries operated by the Kodiak Regional Aquaculture Association through a tax self-imposed by Kodiak's salmon fishermen. Kitoi cultivates a large pink salmon run, but its research emphasis in 1992 was on sockeye. The association's other hatchery at Pillar Creek north of town works with sockeye, and in 1992 efforts focused on turning barren Spiridon Lake into a major sockeye system.

Kodiak's fisheries began diversifying in the 1950s when freezing capabilities came to town, opening new markets. This sparked harvests of red king crab. A few Kodiak salmon fishermen started catching king crab in 1936, testing gear types and exploring markets, mostly for canned crab at the time; Lowell Wakefield, whose family ran a herring plant on Raspberry Island, did much to pioneer the king crab fishery through the 1940s and 1950s. In the 1960s, the king crab fishery exploded in Kodiak.

King crab brought in millions of dollars, but the risks were high. The boats — the earliest ones refitted salmon seiners hardly suited to the open ocean — ventured into the rough open seas, their decks stacked high with steel-framed, nylon-mesh pots. Once at the crabbing grounds, crews worked quickly on rolling, slippery decks to unfasten and bait the pots and loft them over the side. A loose pot could maim or crush a man and more than one took a crew member into the frigid seas. Full pots hoisted back aboard were emptied into the boat's hold, where sea water was pumped to keep the crabs alive. When Kodiak's crabbing was at its peak in the mid-60s, boats might wait days in line to unload at the canneries. The toll was high in boats and lives during the early crabbing years.

The king crab fishery in Kodiak peaked in 1966 with 90 million pounds handled by 32 processors. Two years later, crab helped make Kodiak the top port in the nation in value of product. But stocks were declining and although there was a bit of recovery in the 1970s, the crab boom for Kodiak was ending. The number of processors had dropped to only a dozen or so, several of them

relocating to Dutch Harbor on Unalaska, to be closer to the Bering Sea king crab fishery.

The king crab fishery for Kodiak was closed in 1983, prompting a switch for many into groundfish. The Magnuson Act of 1976 gave Americans priority over fish 200 miles from shore; the first stage in converting to a bottomfishery was joint ventures between American fishermen and the foreign factory fleet. Many of Kodiak's crab fishermen refit their boats for joint ventures, at a cost of $300,000 to $1 million, and retrained their crews. In the meantime, Kodiak's processing plants converted and expanded to handle

The addition of pollock and cod to Kodiak's fishery keeps the town's harbor busy year-round. (David Menke)

pollock and cod, and boat owners again refit their vessels, this time with refrigerated sea water systems to deliver to the shore-based plants.

"When the rest of the state was enjoying the oil boom, Kodiak was in a depression because of the loss of crab, and we were making the painful and expensive transition to groundfish," comments Chris Blackburn.

Kodiak Seafood Processors

ALASKA FRESH SEAFOOD INC.
Owners: Ted Otness of Seattle, company president and product broker; Dave Woodruff of Kodiak, company Alaska operations manager and vice president; brothers Ted and Gary Painter of Oregon, Bering Sea fishermen and former Kodiak crab fishermen; and John Hall, a retired Bering Sea and Kodiak crab fisherman now living in California.
Processes: Halibut, salmon, crab, scallops, sablefish, pollock, cod, Dungeness crab.
History: Company formed in 1978 and bought crab processing facility from North Pacific Processors; as crab stocks dwindled, converted plant into full-line seafood operation with freezer capacity.
Location: 105 Marine Way, Kodiak.
Employs: 12 to 60.

ALASKA PACIFIC SEAFOODS INC.
Owner: Marubeni Corp. of Japan; Alaska Pacific is a division of North Pacific Processors Inc.
Processes: Salmon, halibut, cod, pollock, crab and other Gulf of Alaska and Bering Sea species; also manufactures surimi.
History: Alaska Pacific Seafoods began Kodiak operations in the 1970s, in former Alaska Ice and Cold Storage plant; first shore-based company to make surimi in Alaska, with production initially funded by grant from Alaska Fisheries Development Foundation in 1984; owner Harold Dobinspeck sold company to Marubeni in mid-1980s.
Location: 627 Shelikof, Kodiak. Other North Pacific Processor plants in Cordova, Kenai and Bristol Bay.
Employs: 300 at peak in midsummer; average 130-140 year-round.

ALL ALASKAN SEAFOODS INC.
Owners: Alaska corporation with 20 stockholders; 25 percent held by Hillsdown Seafood, Inc., England.
Processes: Salmon, herring, cod, crab, sablefish, scallops, shrimp, groundfish.
History: Formed in 1976 by Kodiak boat owners Lloyd Cannon, Glenn Evans, Harold Jones, Oscar Dyson and Seldon Nelson, Fred Brechan, Kenny Holland, Bern Hall and Wilburn Hall, Antril Sydan, Ole Harder, Jim Cuthbert and Ken Bowhey. They bought the 385-foot floating mothership *All Alaskan* to process their own catch.

"We were the talk of the waterfront," recalls president and board chairman Lloyd Cannon. "They said we wouldn't last six months, that fishermen couldn't form a company and not be in a total battle."

In 1980, the company bought *Star of Kodiak* from Alaska Packers Association, a subsidiary of Del Monte. Alaska Packers had permanently docked the *Star of Kodiak* liberty ship on the Kodiak waterfront to replace its Halferty cannery, an onshore crab, salmon and clam processing plant that had been destroyed in the 1964 earthquake.

In 1982, All Alaskan Seafoods acquired the 260-foot *Northern Alaska* floating processor to work the burgeoning bottomfish fishery.

In 1987 the Canadian fishing company Clearwater Fine Foods bought into All Alaskan; Hillsdown acquired Clearwater's share in 1988 for settlement of debts.

In 1991, All Alaska Seafoods, with nearly $92 million in revenues, ranked 12th in *Alaska Business Monthly* magazine's listing of largest Alaskan-owned corporations.

Location: *Star of Kodiak*, 111 Marine Way, Kodiak; *All Alaskan* operates in the Bering Sea; *Northern Alaskan* operates in the Bering Sea and Pribilof Islands. Headquarters in Seattle.
Employs: *Star of Kodiak*, 270; *All Alaskan*, 300 during peak season; *Northern Alaskan*, 170 during peak.

CHIGNIK PRIDE FISHERIES
Owner: Sea Catch Inc., Seattle.
Processes: Salmon, halibut, cod, herring, sablefish, groundfish.
History: In operation since 1984; plant previously owned by Peter Pan Foods.
Location: Chignik Bay on the Alaska Peninsula, with offices in Kodiak and Seattle.
Employs: 15 to 20 year-round; 140 during peak season.

EAST POINT SEAFOODS
Owner: Subsidiary of Queen Fisheries Inc., owned by E. H. Bendiksen estate of Seattle.
Processes: Crab, salmon, halibut, bottomfish, sablefish.
History: Started Kodiak operations in 1962, with shrimp processing facilities and space leased from King Crab Inc. and Alaska Ice and Cold

Storage; built own processing plant in 1974; as shrimp declined, diversified to process bottomfish and other species.
Location: 420 Marine Way, Kodiak; also Dutch Harbor, with a Queen Fisheries salmon plant at Dillingham.
Employs: 125 to 150 in season; 15 during off-season.

FAROS (SKOOKUMCHUCK) SEAFOODS

Owner: Family-owned, Massachusetts corporation.
Processes: Frozen and fresh bottomfish fillets.
History: Started operation in Kodiak in 1987 with purchase of Skookumchuck crab plant.
Location: 317 Shelikof, Kodiak; also operates bottomfish plants in Tacoma and Boston.
Employs: 30 to 40 at peak.

INTERNATIONAL SEAFOOD OF ALASKA INC.

Owner: International Oceanic Ent., a subsidiary of Rev. Sun Myung Moon's Unification Church.
Processes: Salmon.
History: $7.5 million plant completed 1980.
Location: 612 Marine Way, Kodiak.
Employs: Company did not provide information.

KING CRAB INC.

Owner: Ocean Beauty Seafoods, Inc., wholly owned subsidiary of Ikamuda Group of Indonesia. Ocean Beauty has processing

facilities in Alaska, Oregon and Washington with distribution and sales throughout the western United States and in Tokyo.
Processes: Bottomfish, sablefish, halibut, crab, salmon, herring.
History: Facilities established 1911 by Kadiak Fisheries; dock and wharf sold to O. Kraft & Son in 1939; cannery buildings requisitioned by military during World War II, then turned over to the city; in 1953, Robert Resoff and Jorgen Fredrickson of Kodiak started Kodiak King Crab, Inc., leasing the city's dock and wharf; taken over by Seattle-based Washington Fish and Oyster in 1954; in mid-1970s, 49.9 percent of Kodiak King Crab owned by Marubeni trading company of Japan; operated by Ocean Beauty Seafoods, a subsidiary of Sealaska Corp. until its sale in 1990 to Ikamuda Group; new cold storage and bottomfish processing facilities added in last six years.
Location: 621 Shelikof, Kodiak. Other Ocean Beauty facilities in Alaska: salmon and herring freezing plant, Naknek; floating crab and salmon processor *Ocean Pride* primarily works Bristol Bay.
Employs: An average of 150 people year-round and 350 people at peak production, Kodiak; 150 people May through August, Naknek plant; 150 to 200 year-round on *Ocean Pride*.

KODIAK SALMON PACKERS

Owner: Privately owned with headquarters in Monroe, Wa.

Processes: all species salmon.
History: Began operations in mid-1980s, in former Alaska Packers Association facilities.
Location: Larsen Bay.
Employment: 160 at peak May to September; caretaker through winter.

SEASIDE SEAFOODS

Owners: Wayne Selby and Bill Bishop, both of Kodiak.
Processes: Custom processing for sports fishermen; small-scale retail and wholesale production of cod, black bass, crab, pollock, salmon.
History: Started operation in mid-1980s as Arctic Choice, located at Middle Bay; about 1990, changed name and moved into town.
Location: 330 Shelikof, Kodiak.
Employs: 3 to 20.

WARDS COVE PACKING CO. INC.

Owner: An Alaska corporation owned by the Brindle family, Alec Brindle president.
Processes: Salmon, halibut, herring, sablefish, Pacific cod.
History: Company started 1928 at Wards Cove north of Ketchikan; purchased Bristol Bay red salmon cannery in 1947; in partnership with Bumblebee Seafoods bought out Libby, McNeil and Libby properties in Alaska in 1959 to operate as Columbia Ward Fisheries, and acquired the Moser Bay plant; expanded to Kodiak in 1964 with purchase of Pacific American Fisheries' Alitak plant; bought Port Bailey plant and Icy

Cape operation on Kodiak's waterfront from Kadiak Fisheries in 1968; the Icy Cape plant was later closed; in mid-1970s, Marubeni Corp., of Japan, bought 20 percent of company; Brindle family bought back Marubeni's share in 1990.
Location: On Kodiak Island, plants at Alitak and Port Bailey; gear storage facility in Moser Bay. Other plants at Ekuk near Dillingham, Excursion Inlet, Kenai, Naknek, Seward, Dutch Harbor and Wards Cove with fish camps at Egegik, Haines, Craig and Hoonah; headquarters in Seattle.
Employs: Seasonally, April through September, with peak employment, 180 to 200 at Alitak; 130 to 150 at Port Bailey.

WESTERN ALASKA FISHERIES

Owner: Taiyo Fisheries, Japan.
Processes: *Bairdi* and *opilio* Tanner crab, king and Dungeness crab, herring, sablefish, halibut, salmon, Pacific cod and pollock fillets, surimi.
History: Established in 1967 by Taiyo as B&B Fisheries to process king crab; name changed to Western Alaska Fisheries in 1979; new plant constructed 1988 for cod and pollock fillets and surimi production.
Location: 521 Shelikof, with headquarters in Seattle.
Employs: average of 80; 180 at peak.

Information was unavailable for **COOK INLET PROCESSING INC.**, Kodiak, owner Tim Blott.

LEFT: *A seiner searches for salmon near Kodiak. Second most valuable of Kodiak's fisheries, the island's salmon industry began in 1882 when Alaska Commercial Co. opened a cannery at the mouth of the Karluk River. (Jim Simmen)*

ABOVE: *Pink salmon, one of the most abundant of Kodiak's salmon, travel along a chute to a processor. Kodiak's pinks come from a variety of sources including the Kitoi Bay Hatchery and the Karluk and Ayakulik rivers. (Jim Simmen)*

"It was a 180-degree turn just when you thought you had your life together. But now Kodiak has made the transition from a major crab port to a major groundfish port."

Recent state surveys of the crab populations show slight improvements, but levels remain depressed. The latest theory, says Dave Jackson with Alaska Department of Fish and Game's division of shellfish, is that perhaps water temperatures are limiting growth of plankton, food for the young. In any event, baby crabs are not growing up. Some red king crab is still

landed at Kodiak from the Bering Sea fishery.

Other crab fisheries continue in Kodiak waters. The most valuable is that of Tanner, or snow, crab. Since 1967, the Tanner fishery has averaged 13 million pounds a year, the high harvest of 33 million pounds occurring in 1978. But Tanner stocks are down, with the lowest harvest of 1.9 million pounds in 1991. Tanner crab started declining in the late 1970s, about the same time populations of its predators such as pollock and cod started increasing. Fisheries biologists think

these occurrences are related. Dungeness crab stocks, a relatively minor fishery for Kodiak, also are depressed. The catch of Dungeness has averaged 3 million pounds a year since 1962, with only 440,000 pounds harvested halfway through the 1992 season. Some fishing also is done for brown king crab, a deep-water species.

Pink shrimp became a major fishery for Kodiak in the 1960s and 1970s, with a high harvest of 82 million pounds in 1971. The last year for a shrimp trawl was in 1985, when the harvest dropped to 1.1 million pounds. Most major production areas are now closed to shrimp trawling, although some offshore areas are open for exploratory shrimp fishing. A few boats in Kodiak fish for spot shrimp with pots, and the few thousand pounds harvested are sold on the fresh market.

Kodiak's herring sac-roe fishery, resurrected in the late 1970s, has blossomed into a lucrative fishery. The 1992 harvest of more than 4,000 tons was the largest on record. Stocks appear healthy and recruits of young herring appear good. The sac-roe fishery, which targets herring during their spawn, runs mid-April through June. A smaller food and bait herring fishery in the fall peaks in October and November.

Scallops, another minor fishery for Kodiak, were being harvested in 1992 by about seven boats that use iron rakes to dredge the sea floor. The peak harvest of 1.4 million pounds of shucked meats occurred in 1970; the 1991 harvest was 683,000 pounds.

A relatively new fishery for Kodiak is for green sea urchins. Sought for their roe, sea urchins are shipped live to Japan. Divers pick the urchins, mostly in October and

November when roe color and sweetness peaks. In 1988, 190,509 pounds were harvested by 28 divers, but in 1991 the harvest dropped to 30,472 pounds with six divers. In late 1991, Mark Blakeslee, a Kodiak sea urchin diver and environmental engineer, conducted a small sea urchin research project, funded by the Alaska Science and Technology Foundation with help from Kodiak Area Native Association and the Fishery Technology Center. The goal was to improve the quality of roe by holding and feeding the urchins in tanks. If successful, urchins could be harvested in calmer, summer seas without the pressure of marketing them within 48 hours of harvest. Blakeslee tried a variety of diets — salmon fry starter, wheat flour and carrots, and agar with flour and salt water to make fake kelp. He found that sea urchins were gluttons, eating 4 to 5 percent of their body weight each day, but he said the project's mixed results were inconclusive as to the feasibility of similar efforts on a commercial scale.

Today, numerous organizations exist — United Fishermen's Marketing Association, Kodiak Longline Vessel Owners Association, Alaska Draggers Association, Alaska Groundfish Data Bank, Kodiak Island Seiners Association — to help fishermen do their jobs better and, in the case of the UFMA, negotiate prices. Kodiak's fishermen are an independent and often cantankerous bunch who rarely agree. But occasionally they unite in a powerful way. A complaint from Kodiak's processors and fishermen in 1989 that the offshore factory fleet was taking their groundfish quota resulted in a change to federal fisheries law in 1992. Led

by the longliners, Kodiak's fishing community in 1991 and 1992 fought a federal plan to impose "individual fishing quotas" in the halibut and black cod fisheries. These IFQs would restrict the number of halibut and block cod fishermen to those with proven past participation. Those from Kodiak argued against IFQs on economic, biological and social grounds. They contended IFQs are a prescription for bankruptcy by limiting fishermen's flexibility and making access to the fisheries expensive, assuming permits would even be available. In late 1992, a final decision was pending.

OTHER INDUSTRIES: PAST AND PRESENT
Fishing keeps Kodiak going, but the landscape is not devoid of other activities. Logging, tourism and sport hunting are part

Bill Burton has run Kodiak Cattle Ranch at Narrow Cape with wife Kathy and son Buck since 1967. For decades ranchers have tried to build a thriving cattle industry on the Kodiak archipelago, but natural hazards such as cliffs, tideflats, poison hemlock, grass devoid of nutrients in winter and bears have thwarted these efforts for the most part. Burton plans to replace most of his cattle with buffalo and turn his ranch into a game ranch. (Roz Goodman)

Kodiak's growing tourism industry has spawned a number of lodges, some on the road system like Kalsin Bay Inn, and some in remote corners of the archipelago. Small cruise ships are now putting in at Kodiak, and visitors to the downtown tourist information center have increased 114 percent from 1991 to July 1992. (Don Pitcher)

bowheads in the northern seas. A Norwegian shore-based whaling group expanded their Akutan operations to Port Hobron on Sitkalidak Island in 1917. In 1925, the American Pacific Whaling Co. operated out of Port Hobron, selling whale meat, salted and packed in barrels for 10 cents a pound.

The Russians also introduced fox farming, bringing blue fox to the islands. The Americans continued, and island leasing in the early 1900s by the U.S. Forest Service included parcels at Raspberry Straits and on Afognak Island. The best pelt prices, about $100 each, came before the big depression of the 1930s, which put most fur farmers out of business.

Perhaps the most unusual enterprise was ice harvesting on Woody Island in the 1850s. For a few years, ice from Tanignak Lake cooled drinks from California to South America. Until that time, ice came to California from Boston around Cape Horn. The San Francisco Ice Co. started in Sitka, but moved operations to Woody Island in 1857 where the ice grew as thick as 18 inches in the coldest winters. The company built a storehouse to hold 15,000 tons of ice insulated in sawdust. Natives who hunted sea otters in the summer spent winters cutting ice, dropping the blocks on a flume that delivered the ice to the storehouse and wharf. In the beginning they were paid 12 cents a day, along with a noon meal of fish soup and rye bread and a nip of vodka three times a day. The company also brought some of the first horses to Alaska, to use in the ice harvest, and built Alaska's first road around the island to exercise the animals during the summer. The ice business out of

of the mix. Ranching continues, with some of the herds giving ground to buffalo, and on a much smaller scale than years ago when promoters billed Kodiak as a cattleman's heaven. To look at what has gone on through the years, how people have

made their way in the islands, is to see a curious assortment of adaptations.

Kodiak hung on the fringe of the heavily hunted Northwest Right Whaling Grounds of the 1800s. The Russians took whales in the late 1700s, assigning Natives to hunt from their bidarkas in the bays of Kodiak and Afognak islands. A favorite Russian dish was pavlina — fresh belly meat steamed, preserved in fish roe, cooked in sour berries and packed into barrels. By 1835, New England whalemen seeking oil and baleen found sperm and right whales in the Gulf of Alaska waters around Kodiak, and the hunting here preluded the rush for

Woody Island was brisk, the first shipments bringing 25 cents a pound. The market for Alaska ice cooled with invention of an ice-making machine and completion of the Central Pacific Railroad, linking San Francisco with icy lakes in the Sierra Nevadas. Inventors of the ice machine were so anxious to market their contraption that they paid the ice company to not ship ice from Alaska, according to Yule Chaffin in *Alaska's Konyag Country* (1983). In turn, the ice company kept cutting and storing ice to ensure that the ice machine manufacturers would not renege on their contract.

Cattle ranching in the archipelago generally has shown more promise than profitability. At its height, Kodiak's cattle industry numbered a few thousand animals; today Kodiak Island has about 600 head, according to one of the few remaining ranchers. Several hundred more cattle are located on Sitkinak, Sitkalidak and Chirikof islands with a few head on Harvester and Bear islands. A picturesque remnant of Kodiak's herds are the small shaggy cows from Northland Ranch at Kalsin Bay that often clog the road between Kodiak and Chiniak.

Visitors even in Russian times lauded the place as good for cattle, with good grasslands and a moderate climate. The Russians brought the first cows, Siberian stock, in 1794 and tended about 300 at the time of American purchase. About 80 remained in 1900 and in one attempt to restock the island, a Seattle meat-packing plant landed 200 Herefords; 140 died the first winter. The U.S. Agricultural Department's experiment station brought 50 Galloway cattle to Kalsin Bay in 1907 and the herd did fine until

Novarupta blasted the place, covering the grass with ash. Efforts continued through the 1920s and 1930s, even after the experiment station moved to Matanuska Valley in 1931. By 1939, three ranchers had about 350 cattle. The number of cattle had almost tripled by 1956 on nine government leases, and in 1965 the herds numbered more than 1,300.

As ranchers turned their animals loose to range on large government leasing tracts,

BELOW: *Since 1987 Sea-Land Freight has provided twice weekly containership service to Kodiak from the Lower 48. The 710-foot* Sea-Land Kodiak *was built specifically for the Alaska trade. (Matt Johnson)*

RIGHT: *The Crab Festival Grand Parade winds along Rezanof Drive through downtown Kodiak. The festival, first held years ago to celebrate the end of king crab season, remains an annual May event even though the king crab fishery around Kodiak is closed. In spring 1992, state-owned Rezanof Drive erupted with potholes, prompting locals to joke that anyone who drove the road without weaving was probably drunk. (Marion Stirrup)*

they discovered some drawbacks in this cattlemen's paradise: Cattle fell off cliffs, became mired in tideflats, died from eating poison hemlock. The abundant red-top grass fattened the cattle, true, but turned nutritionally void in winter. Haymaking was good when weather permitted, which could be infrequent, and costs for importing supplemental grain were high.

Then there are the bears. Ranchers have been blaming losses on bears since the

1930s; an Alaska Game Commission study in 1939 said they were exaggerating the problem, when in most cases the bears were just feeding on cattle that had died from other causes. But Bill Burton, who has been operating the Kodiak Cattle Ranch since 1967 with wife Kathy and son Buck, says bears have always been a problem and have gotten worse in recent years.

High winds rake a fishing boat in Kodiak's harbor. Wind, rain and moderate temperatures typify the archipelago's weather. Kodiak averages 74 inches of rain annually, with temperatures averaging 50 to 60 degrees in summer and the low 20s in winter. (Jim Simmen)

The Burtons lease 20,000 acres from the Bureau of Land Management at Narrow Cape, 50 miles southeast of town on the road system. He figures bears have killed about 25 head of his herd a year. The bear problem, along with low prices for cattle and high costs for feed and transportation, are the reason he has switched to raising buffalo. They stand up better against bears, he says. He keeps about 75 head of cattle, enough to supply the rodeo each August during the Kodiak State Fair. He hopes to increase his 150 buffalo to about 400, and has basically turned his working cattle ranch into a game ranch. He hosts buffalo hunts, sells buffalo meat, and offers horse riding and horse packing trips for sport fishing,

deer and bear hunting. On top of this, he plans to add elk to the mix. Omar Stratman, another long-time cattleman and owner of Northland Ranch, likewise has tapped the tourism market with guest bunkhouses, trail rides and the like.

Tourism is flourishing in Kodiak. In July 1992, the number of people coming into the downtown visitor's center was up 114 percent over the year before, reports Lois Hansen, executive director of the Kodiak Island Convention and Visitors Bureau. "People are finding out about us," Hansen says. "We're a little more difficult to reach, but that's in our favor because we don't have millions of people and congestions of autos."

Kodiak's visitors span the gamut — sightseers, hunters, sport fishermen, adventure seekers, history buffs. They arrive on 12 commercial flights a day out of Anchorage and the state ferry. From town, they can charter boats and planes to wilderness lodges, remote park service cabins, or to see bears in Kodiak National Wildlife Refuge.

For the first time in 1992, Kodiak hosted small cruise ships catering to "ecotourism." Ecotourism, the latest trend in the industry, stresses appreciation without consumption; that is, look and enjoy but do not disturb. These cruises feature staff naturalists and offer outings in kayaks or inflatable Zodiacs. Kodiak wildlife and miles of shoreline make it a good destination for such folks, says Hansen, adding that birders make up another growing segment of visitors. Kodiak's bear, deer and elk populations are well-known among hunters, as are its rivers and streams among fishermen. Kodiak fishing guides expect even more clients

because of increasing pressures on the popular Kenai Peninsula sport fisheries.

Logging on Afognak Island became a basic industry with significance to Kodiak with the Alaska Native Claims Settlement Act of 1971. With that act, 13 Native corporations became owners of land on Afognak. Today, two Native logging ventures representing those corporations cut Sitka spruce at a steady rate. Most of the logs are exported to China and Japan, although a few shipments beginning in 1991 went to domestic mills. The U.S. Forest Service values Afognak's timber industry at $17 to $20 million a year.

A small amount of logging occurred previously on Afognak. In 1968, when the island was still part of Chugach National Forest, the forest service held the Perenosa timber sale. Strong opposition to the sale came from Kodiak, from people who wanted the logs processed in Kodiak, and from biologists and conservationists who questioned the effect logging would have on the environment and wildlife habitat. Some logging eventually took place under modified terms of the sale.

During World War II, the military cut lumber on Afognak for building bases mostly in the Aleutians. The military occupied a site on Danger Bay now used by Ben A. Thomas Inc., the logging company for Afognak Native Corp. that also logs lands owned by Afognak Joint Venture (AJV), a Native-owned company composed of Koniag Inc. regional corporation, Afognak Native Corp., and seven other village corporations. A wheel from the military's sawmill is still visible at low tide; some of the mill was moved close to Afognak village where it operated until the earthquake and tidal wave.

Koncor Forest Products, a joint venture of four village corporations including Ouzinkie and Natives of Kodiak, manages the other Afognak Island timber operation.

The logging of Afognak has generated some opposition from Kodiak residents and others who object to clear-cutting old growth forests. Even some Native shareholders have mixed feelings about seeing trees harvested from ancestral lands. However, the corporations are mandated to return profits to shareholders; to achieve this

LEFT: *Disposing of garbage presents problems for island communities with limited landfill space. In 1990, the Kodiak Island Borough started shipping aluminum, cardboard, newsprint and white paper to recycling plants off the island. Glass is crushed and used as fill material in the landfill. Stacy Studebaker, a former National Park Service ranger turned high school biology teacher, came up with an alternative use for waste glass and built this 120-foot-long glass bottle-concrete wall on her property. (Marion Stirrup)*

ABOVE: *Wayne McCrary cuts a turkey, while his wife, J.B., and children Alexander (left) and Caitlin gather around the table The McCrary family lives on remote Chirikof Island, and had just received Thanksgiving supplies when this photo was taken in December 1990. (Bob Hallinen,* Anchorage Daily News*)*

they use approved timber management practices to optimize their resource base. Both leave trees standing along streams and lakes in buffers often wider than required by law. Often they leave marginal stands of trees on the edge of clear-cuts, which

ABOVE: *Native-owned timber leaves Afognak Island on ships that load in Danger Bay. Logs are sorted and graded in the yard, then rafted in the water until pickup. (Koncor Forest Products)*

RIGHT: *A swing yarder works a clear-cut area on Afognak Island. (Koncor Forest Products)*

provides a variety of wildlife habitats. Sitka deer and Roosevelt elk browse the clear-cuts.

The Afognak group and Koncor differ somewhat in their approach. AJV would like to ultimately sell back about 125,000 acres of its timbered and non-timbered holdings to the government, and has lobbied for several projects to assess the resources of its land. In summer 1992, the U.S. Fish and Wildlife Service was conducting a habitat and species study that included research on the marbled murrelet; Alaska Fish and Game was doing a fish study; and Afognak Joint Venture had funded a plant inventory. During the next decade, the state and federal governments

will receive $1 billion from the Exxon Corp. as part of the *Exxon Valdez* oil spill settlement, and AJV wants part of that money used to put Afognak land back in the public domain. The corporation would use its payment to set up a permanent fund for shareholders.

Koncor, in contrast, plans to keep its land for logging and in 1992 joined the American Tree Farm system. Koncor president John Sturgeon figures the company has another 25 to 30 years of logging ahead. Its harvest has ranged from 10 to 35 million board feet a year. Since Koncor started logging here in

1977, it has planted more than a million seedlings in a reforestation program. In addition to planting seedlings by hand, Koncor uses helicopters to broadcast spruce seed over clear-cuts. It also is planting seed stock from Juneau, which grows faster and straighter than the native stock. Koncor plans to build cabins and perhaps a lodge in the future to tap into tourism. Afognak Native Corp., likewise, has attempted to diversify somewhat into tourism through its subsidiary Afognak Adventures, which has operated recreational cabins on the island since 1986.

Janet Axell, Setnetter

BY IRVING WARNER

Editor's note: *Kodiak writer Irving Warner has had numerous articles published, and has received a National Endowment for the Arts Fellowship in Fiction. He is working on a screenplay, and teaches at the Kodiak campus of the University of Alaska.*

Each May Janet Axell navigates her skiff down the west side of Kodiak Island, edging cautiously along stormy Shelikof Strait. When she comes in view of her setnet site, she experiences a moment of renewal.

"In the distance I can see Cape Uganik. Every year it just gives me that feel-good sensation all over."

Janet's setnet site, instead of being in sheltered inside waters, is at the cape. With an 80-foot bluff at her back, and a willful and forbidding Shelikof Strait to the front, her site is an embattled ribbon of rock-strewn beach.

The site's cabins are accessible via a steep trail. Every can of beans — every household item for three months of living — must travel up that precipice on either Janet's back or those of her two assistants. Though Janet is not one to complain, an outsider readily surmises that after 90 days of round trips up that bluff, both spirit and legs surely become strong and robust.

On the beach below, the powerful surf pounds Cape Uganik ceaselessly. During a salmon opening, Janet and crew must fish through all but the worst of it.

Despite these physical extremes, Janet has come to have a special feeling about this brooding, raw seascape. "At Cape Uganik, it is wild and alive. It's special."

A glance at Janet, 51, is an accurate chronicle of a decade-plus of weather and tides that daily menace Cape Uganik. They have sculpted her Nordic features with the marks of a hundred storms. More importantly, the rugged, wearing weather has become part of the way she views the world. Janet shrugs off the grayest Kodiak day with an almost undetectable rise of her shoulders. The unforgiving weather has strengthened the native Minnesotan's skills at accepting things — human and climatic — for the way they are.

Yet it is the hands that tell the clearest story.

Janet Axell sorts through salmon at her setnet site on Cape Uganik. (Marion Stirrup)

When she reaches for a cup of tea, her strong, capable hands show the tough, endless work of pulling hard against kelp-laden lines, and being thrust thousands of times into wet, clammy gloves, then picking fish and debris from her net.

Janet's sojourn to a life of fishing was

circuitous. Along the way there were numerous choices. Her story is like that of many Alaskans who migrated north in the 1960s after completing their college education.

"I drove to Alaska by myself. My husband preceded me north by several weeks. The minute I got here, I felt I belonged in Alaska — it was home."

Pre-pipeline Alaska, its raw wilderness, the solitude and resident iconoclasm captivated her. At that moment, Janet abandoned forever a comfortably urban or suburban existence. The Alaska-Canada border became her Rubicon.

By the mid-1970s, Janet's marriage was firmly archived. Yet already she had had her introduction to commercial fishing. "I began by fishing halibut in Kodiak in 1973. In those days, of course, the seasons lasted for weeks, even months."

After seven years of crab, shrimp and halibut fishing, Janet opted out of big stakes commercial fishing. In 1980, she purchased the setnet site on Uganik Island.

"I love the ocean and the land, so it is a nice combination of the two. Plus, I don't want the responsibility of a big boat breaking down."

Her thoughts about Cape Uganik are an interesting blend of Renoir impressionism and Wyeth seascapes.

"Some nights when there are high waves breaking on the beach, their natural phosphorescence is so white. Once out on the water, I feel like I'm being transported through a galaxy into another world."

When she is asked about opting out of the American Dream — the house in the suburbs and creature comforts — she at first hesitates. But when she hears herself described as colorful, Janet is finally prodded to discuss the choices she has made.

"I don't think a person looks at themselves as being colorful. And the other stuff. Well, as a woman, I imagine that was what I was supposed to do. But my spirit just never fit the confinement of that kind of image."

In April 1989, Janet and other Kodiakans were abruptly shocked out of their peaceful seasonal routine when the *Exxon Valdez* ripped open on Bligh Reef.

A barrage of television clips from Prince William Sound became emblematic of that tragedy for all America. Because of these, few off island realized how dramatically the ugly flotillas of sticky mouse outraged the west side of Kodiak Island. Janet articulates her feelings with dismay.

"I cleaned oil for about a month at the cape. Watching how the people reacted made me terribly sad. All the bad human

The Alaska Peninsula across Shelikof Strait frames this view of Janet Axell's setnet site on Cape Uganik. (Marion Stirrup)

feelings resulting because of the spill were almost as harmful as what the oil did."

Instead of dwelling on the tragic events of 1989, Janet prefers to switch the subject to one of the numerous experiences she has been privileged to have at Cape Uganik. Her clear favorite is the whale's tail incident.

She warms to the telling quickly.

"Several summers ago, my niece Laura was one of my helpers. I'd promised her whales all summer, but we'd seen none. Finally, just beyond the end of the net we heard one blow."

Janet, an expert whale watcher, quickly identified it as an adult humpback. While they watched, the leviathan surfaced repeatedly, staying uncharacteristically close to the site.

"I noticed a stray crab-pot buoy nearby. At the cape, this isn't unusual. But soon I realized it wasn't a stray, rather it was attached by a long line to the whale."

The whale was now surfacing with unusual frequency. Clearly it was badly fatigued. "Finally I told Laura, 'I think the whale wants us to take the buoy off.' When we got into the skiff and approached it, it didn't spook. Instead, it surfaced right in front of us. Positioning itself. Its tail was right beside us."

Despite Laura's fears concerning their humanitarian venture, Janet brought the skiff within a few feet of the huge mammal's formidable flukes.

Despite the danger in bringing aboard a tangled knot of crab line attached to this 30-ton giant, Janet persisted.

"I felt confident that the whale knew what had to be done. Laura grabbed the buoy while I maneuvered, and we hauled in

Janet Axell began her Kodiak fishing career in the halibut fishery in 1973. She switched to setnet fishing seven years later. (Marion Stirrup)

about 80 feet of crab line, then the buoy. We cut if off about 10 feet from its flukes. We could see raw skin around the tail. It couldn't have dragged all that line and buoy around much longer."

Now free of the buoy and almost all the line, the humpback dove immediately and was on its way. "You could tell," says Janet with satisfaction ". . . that after we got the line off, it was able to stay down much longer."

Though such a daring act of mercy is not recommended for ordinary sorts, the event typified the spiritual connection Janet feels with all living things. It is part of what makes her unique.

Defining precisely what makes her such an original personality is difficult. But surely Janet's spirit is constructed from the most

ancient of elements — earth, air, water and fire. The first three are her everyday companions at Cape Uganik. The last, fire, is not something any of her friends might associate with the normally sedate Janet. But it certainly has its place in the process.

A person cannot become as independent and special as Janet without becoming hardened and polished by the fires of a rigorous forge. Perhaps it was this process that melted away numerous bonds that restrain so many of us. Deep within Janet freedom and individualism have become brother and sister.

Kodiak's Fishery Industrial Technology Center

LEFT: *The $7.5 million Fishery Industrial Technology Center on Near Island, opposite Kodiak town, is an arm of the University of Alaska's School of Fisheries and Ocean Science. (Marion Stirrup)*

BELOW: *Bill Osborne pours fish meal into a specialized grinder, an example of the high technology equipment supporting research at the University of Alaska's Fishery Industrial Technology Center. Waste Alaska pollock is ground and dried into fish meal, which is in turn used to produce animal feed. (Hank Pennington)*

The Fishery Industrial Technology Center in Kodiak brings Alaska's seafood industry into a new era. Research projects underway here could result in better fish harvesting methods, improved fish processing techniques and new seafood products.

The fish tech center — the seafood and fishing technology arm of University of Alaska's School of Fisheries and Ocean Science — opened its seafood science building in 1991, nearly a decade after entering its first temporary office above Tony's Bar. The seafood industry lags far behind the poultry, pork and beef industries in developing new products and markets, so the fish tech center has its work cut out. While other universities have larger food science research centers in the United States, UAF's Fishery Industrial Technology Center brings together the most seafood specialists. Its location in

Kodiak taps into the tons of fresh seafood coming ashore annually.

The center could enhance Alaska's long-term goal of marketing value-added seafood products. Currently most Alaska fish is exported whole, or as frozen fillets or surimi. Further processing of fish before it leaves the state would make it more valuable, and research at the fish tech center may help make that possible. "The potential uses of fish protein are only beginning to be tapped," says John French, center director. "There's a great variety of value-added products and many should be consumer-ready. The American public likes something that doesn't take a lot of time and preparation. American consumers tend to shy away from fish because they don't know how to prepare it."

The $7.5 million facility on Near Island includes a pilot plant for developing and testing seafood processing operations. Fundamental and applied research takes place in biochemistry, chemistry, engineering and microbiology laboratories. A kitchen with individual testing stations allows taste, smell and texture evaluations of new fish products. The center's projects are supported by industry, and state and federal grants.

The center's staff of fisheries biologists, food scientists, seafood engineers and microbiologists do a variety of work in four main areas: fish harvesting, seafood processing, fisheries and food science training, and transferring technology to the fishing industry and state and federal agencies.

Recent research activities include:

• Evaluating *sous-vide* processing for pink salmon. This European process yields a pasteurized, seasoned entreé that is vacuum-packed in a pouch, which can then be boiled or zapped in a microwave to serve. *Sous-vide* processed products are used in the United States by some large hotel chains.

• Developing extrusion processing of salmon muscle proteins.

• Evaluating opportunities for flaked products from pink salmon.

• Surveying the microbiological quality of Alaska seafood.

• Technical support and technology development for pollock surimi manufacturing.

• Improving chilled and refrigerated seawater systems for fishing vessels and tenders.

• Analysis of flatfish reactions to rig trawls to minimize halibut by-catch through the use of modified trawl gear.

• Identifying new methods for detecting and removing parasites in white fish.

• Evaluating handling, quality and stability of whole and minced flatfish.

• Characterization of seafood processing by-products for conversion to energy and other products.

Starting in 1993, graduate courses in food science may be offered in addition to undergraduate courses currently taught by the center's faculty and research staff of a dozen scientists.

Plans call for expanding the fisheries science, fish harvesting technology, and seafood safety programs at the center. These would be expanded into a multi-agency fisheries research complex that would also house National Marine Fisheries Service and Alaska Department of Fish

TOP LEFT: *A goal of the Alaska fishing industry is to expand beyond traditional canned or whole-frozen markets for pink salmon. Chuck Crapo (white shirt) and Brian Himelbloom prepare pink salmon using European* sous-vide *processing methods, where the salmon is vacuum sealed in consumer-ready pouches, frozen, then steam cooked before serving. (Hank Pennington)*

ABOVE: *Mark Blakeslee places green sea urchins in rearing pens for evaluation of growth rates and diets. (Hank Pennington)*

and Game employees in Kodiak. The expansion would include a gravity-fed seawater system, wet and dry research laboratories, classrooms and a fisheries and seafood library.

Largest U.S. Coast Guard Base

The U.S. Coast Guard operates its largest base on Kodiak. Its presence contributes significantly to the economy of Kodiak, the safety of fishermen in Alaska's northern oceans, enforcement of maritime law, and aids air and sea navigation from the west coast of Canada to the east coast of Russia.

About 1,000 Coast Guardsmen and 1,500 family members live on Kodiak, mostly in military housing on base. A tour-of-duty on Kodiak ranges from 18 months to three years. The base generates an annual payroll of about $41 million, of which more than $2.5 million goes to civilian personnel and nearly $3 million to private contractors.

The Coast Guard first arrived in Kodiak in 1947, as an air detachment on the Naval Air Station. In 1972, the Navy decommissioned its base and the Coast Guard took over. Today, the USCG Support Center Kodiak encompasses 23,000 acres of land. It is the Coast Guard's only support center serving both cutters and aircraft. In addition, the base in Kodiak covers nine other units:

• *Storis*, a 230-foot medium endurance cutter with primary missions of search and rescue, fisheries patrol and

law enforcement. The *Storis* served in Greenland during World War II and was assigned to Alaska in 1949. Its crew consists of nine officers and 63 enlisted personnel.

•*Yocona*, a 213-foot cutter used primarily for maritime law enforcement and search and rescue. Commissioned by the Navy in 1944 as the USS *Seize*, it came to the Coast Guard in 1946. It is crewed by 10 officers and 70 enlisted personnel.

• *Ironwood,* an 180-foot buoy-tender that formerly homeported in

This aerial looks west across the U.S. Coast Guard base in Kodiak toward Old Womens Mountain. The base was built during World War II for Navy use; in the foreground is one of three military runways built here at that time. The red-roofed Coast Guard Support Center administration building marks the main entrance to the base off Rezanof Drive. The three large hangars at the head of Old Womens Bay, left center, make up the Air Station, one of 10 Coast Guard commands located here. The road along Women's Bay at the foot of the mountain passes the docks of Samson Tug and Barge Co. and Lash Corp. as it continues south to Chiniak. (Frank P. Flavin)

ABOVE: *C-130 airplanes and H-65 helicopters, like these shown, along with H-3 helicopters are assigned to Air Station Kodiak. In 1992, an H-3 Coast Guard helicopter crew from Kodiak won a National Naval Helicopter Association Award for the heroic rescue of four fishermen from the* Dora H., *which sank May 8, 1991, during a storm. The helicopter arrived at the scene shortly after midnight. Using night-vision goggles, the crew spotted a life raft riding 35-foot seas. Rescue swimmer Aviation Survivalman 3rd Class Gary Strebe was lowered by sling but as he hit the water, a swell knocked away his mask and snorkel. He swam through heavy seas to the raft and began taking survivors one at a time 30 yards from the raft to be lifted aboard in a basket. Meanwhile, pilot Lt. Cmdr. Clifford Comer and co-pilot Lt. j.g. Bob Yerex held the helicopter steady in 45-knot winds for the next 45 minutes to perform four hoists. Strebe came up with the last hoist, afraid the weather would make a fifth attempt impossible. Other crew included Aviation Structural Mechanic 2nd Class Jeff Waite and Aviation Electrician's Mate 2nd Class Dave Schron. A C-130 airplane provided cover during the rescue. (Jim Simmen)*

RIGHT: *This view shows the main gate and the Coast Guard Support Center administration building looking east toward Cliff Point. (Don Pitcher)*

Homer and Adak. Its primary mission is maintaining navigational lights and buoys in the Aleutians, Bering Sea and Bristol Bay. It has a crew of 56.

• *Firebrush*, a 180-foot buoytender that formerly served in the North Atlantic. Its primary mission is maintaining navigation aids from Afognak Island to the southwest tip of the Alaska Peninsula. Her crew also numbers 56.

• Air Station Kodiak, which supports all Coast Guard missions including search and rescue, enforcement of laws and treaties, particularly those relating to the U.S. 200-mile Fisheries Conservation Zone, military readiness and air resupply and support for isolated units. Assigned to the air station are six C-130 airplanes, four H-3 helicopters, four H-65 helicopters and nearly 400 people in flying,

maintenance and support roles.

• Communication Station Kodiak, the largest Coast Guard communications facility in both land area and number of personnel. Originally a Coast Guard radio station, it was established in 1957. Its staff of more than 100 handles the majority of Coast Guard communications in the North Pacific.

• LORAN-C Station Kodiak, which includes a monitor site at Spruce Cape and a 625-foot transmitter tower at Narrow Cape. The tower, in conjunction with towers at Shoal Creek, Tok and Port Clarence, provide information to military and civilian navigators in the air and water of the Gulf of Alaska and Bering Sea. The

Spruce Cape site monitors and controls Gulf of Alaska and North Pacific LORAN-C chains. The LORAN station is staffed by 27 people.

• Electronic Support Unit Kodiak, commissioned in 1990 to handle all aspects of Coast Guard electronics, except computers.

• Marine Safety Detachment, which is a subunit of the Marine Safety Office Anchorage and staffed by one officer and one petty officer. Kodiak's detachment inspects commercial vessels, does vessel casualty investigations, conducts marine environmental protection missions and performs port safety and law enforcement in the Kodiak Island area.

Shuyak Island, Distant Jewel

BY ANDY HALL

Editor's note: *After stints as a reporter for the* Kodiak Daily Mirror *and* The Anchorage Times, *Andy has returned to Kodiak to work for the local newspaper.*

At the northern tip of the Kodiak archipelago lies Shuyak Island. Surrounded on three sides by waters of the Gulf of Alaska and Shelikof Strait and by Afognak Island to the south, Shuyak's remote location has discouraged all but the slightest intrusion by modern man. A closer look reveals an island unique in physiography and rich in history.

Shuyak Island is small, just 11 miles by 14 miles, with flat terrain boasting a high point of only about 600 feet. Its flatness can be attributed to heavy glaciation when the

A kayaker tends his gear near the ranger station at Big Bay on the west side of Shuyak Island. Kayaking or other water transportation is about the best way to explore the island because thick vegetation makes overland passage difficult. (Michael L. Goodwin)

polar ice cap extended well south of the archipelago and completely covered Shuyak. When the ice retreated and sea level rose, about 10,000 years ago, water filled the glacial valleys, creating a rugged coastline with more protected waterways than any other island in the Kodiak group.

The island itself is covered with a thick forest of Sitka spruce that arrived relatively recently, 800 to 1,000 years ago. During the summer a heavy undergrowth thrives in the forest consisting of devil's club, blue joint and beach rye grass, dogwood, Sitka alder, salmonberry, wild rose, highbush cranberry, spiraea, willow, ferns, mosses and lichens.

Animal life on the island consists of brown bear, red fox and Sitka blacktail deer. Red foxes were native to the island, but all were wiped out, primarily by use of poison bait, in the early 20th century. Blue foxes were introduced also by Russian fur traders seeking to establish a permanent population of furbearers. The U.S. government transplanted deer to the island for hunting. Dall porpoises, harbor seals, sea lions and sea otters commonly occur in waters surrounding the island.

Sitka spruce surround Mulcahy View Cabin on Neketa Bay, one of four public use cabins within Shuyak Island State Park. (Michael L. Goodwin)

Migrating waterfowl like oldsquaw and harlequin ducks; Steller's and king eiders; common murres; murrelets; and surf, white-winged and common scoters occupy coastal waters. Shuyak's land birds include the bald eagle, belted kingfisher, raven, crow, magpie and downy woodpecker.

On a good day the peaks of northwestern Afognak Island are visible looking south from Neketa Bay on Shuyak Island. Shuyak is accessible by boat or plane from Kodiak or Homer. The 44,288-acre island is 54 air miles north of Kodiak. (Michael L. Goodwin)

A variety of sport fish can be found in the island's streams and bays including rainbow trout, Dolly Varden, pink and silver salmon.

Shuyak once was home to a large population of Koniags, a Native group linguistically linked to the Eskimo. These people plied the waters of the archipelago in bidarkas, relying mostly on sea mammals and fish for food.

The historical record of the Shuyak people is limited but clearly shows a strong-willed, defiant people who did not yield easily to Russian intrusion.

In 1778, the famous British navigator Capt. James Cook landed on Kodiak Island for ship repairs at Snug Corner Cove, near Three Saints Bay. His meetings with the Natives were friendly, although he described them as "inclined to thievery" and unacquainted with firearms. When he departed, he mistakenly charted Kodiak, Afognak and Shuyak islands as part of the mainland.

Soon after the Russian fur hunters established a presence on Kodiak Island, they encountered the people of Shuyak Island. In 1784 Grigorii Shelikov established the first permanent settlement on Kodiak Island at Three Saints Bay. A year later he focused his attention on the outlying islands and had his first exchange with the inhabitants of Shuyak. Trade goods were entrusted to the Toyon, or chief, of Shuyak for purchase of furs during the winter and, as was customary, the Natives left hostages with the Russians.

In an incident reported by I.A. Pil, acting Governor General of Irkutsk and Koyyvan in 1789, some Shuyak chiefs came to Kodiak to visit their hostage children. Two Russians were sent back with them, taking small trading goods. Two Natives from Afognak Island later related to other Natives (who subsequently reported to Shelikov) that the Shuyaks killed the two Russians.

Shelikov killed the two informants and, "(s)ent Russians in three baidaras to Afognak and Shuyak to kill the natives and find the chief to whom the Russians had been sent." Reports came back that all the Natives from one settlement were killed and that residents of other villages had run off.

There is also a report that the Shuyak Toyon called for a force of 1,000 men from the Chugach and Kenai tribes of the mainland to try to destroy Shelikov's settlement, but the war party dispersed without attacking. It is not clear if this force was gathered before or after Shelikov's attack.

The following spring, Shelikov established a fort on Afognak Island, across from Shuyak, and little is heard of the Shuyak people again.

On April 9, 1803, a group of 200 bidarkas assembled at Shuyak Island to wait for Russian hunting supervisors. They reported there were no permanent inhabitants on Shuyak at that time but that "the islanders visit there to hunt seals and sea lions."

In 1965, Ted Chemavisky, then 50 years old, was interviewed by Yule Chaffin and said that his grandfather had lived on Shuyak in 1841, and that "(o)ne whole end of Shuyak Island had been a huge native village but that there was not much of it even then (1841)."

The fate of the Shuyak Islanders is unclear but attack and subjugation by Shelikov as well as diseases brought to the island by the Russians probably contributed to their disappearance.

In the early part of the 20th century human activity on the island picked up again as salmon and herring fisheries expanded in the area.

Neal Sargent of Kodiak, now 72, lived as a boy at Big Bay on Shuyak where his father, Fred Sargent, operated a salmon salting business. Sargent recalls that in 1925 four herring plants operated in the Raspberry Straits area and several floating processors moved into the water off Shuyak Island.

In 1930, Peter Wold and his manager, John Torwik, converted a herring saltery into a one-line cannery and formed Port Williams Packing Co. They put up 8,500 cases the first season, then did not operate until 1934, when they came under the management of Seattle-based Washington Fish and Oyster Co. The Port Williams facility stopped canning in the 1960s, but kept the cold storage going until 1976. That year Wayne and Kay Treat, commercial fishermen from Kodiak, purchased the Port Williams buildings and moved there.

Today the island is generally uninhabited. The cannery still stands at Port Williams, but it has been converted into a fishing and sightseeing lodge. During the winter its only inhabitant is a caretaker. The Federal Aviation Agency operated a repeater station about 10 miles from Port Williams, but this facility has been shut down. Neil Sargent and a few others have cabins on the island, but there are no year-round inhabitants.

Eleven thousand acres of the island are now a state park that offers wilderness camping with four public use cabins located on Big Bay, Carry Inlet and Neketa Bay. Few trails exist and overland travel is difficult because of the heavy undergrowth of devil's club. Foot travel is easiest along the beaches, but these can be covered at high tide .

Sea kayaking is becoming popular in the intricate bays and inlets. Ironically, modern man is rediscovering the island in much the same way that the island's original inhabitants saw it.

A wave- and wind-swept coastline covered with vegetation grading from tundra to Sitka spruce forests characterizes much of Shuyak's western shore. This view looks west across Shelikof Strait to Cape Douglas and the Alaska Peninsula. (Michael L. Goodwin)

The Bears of Kodiak

The only thing some people know about Kodiak are stories of its giant bears. No wonder images of them abound — on brochures, hats, T-shirts, statues, and in public places where dead bears in glass cases lurch forward with swiping claws and snarling teeth. They are its most famous denizens.

The mystique of Kodiak bears translates to big business. Hundreds of visitors come each year to hunt bears with cameras and guns. In 1990 for instance, 21,300 people visited the Kodiak National Wildlife Refuge and visitation was expected to be up in 1992. Wilderness lodges, charter boats and flying services cater to these bear-seekers. One company sells bear-viewing flights with money-back guarantees for no-show bears. Bear guides charge $10,000 or more to take clients on wilderness hunts. The nine public-use cabins within the refuge are booked

These cubs, with their mother at Dog Salmon Creek, display a white collar which will fade by the spring of their second year. (Valeria Martin Menke)

months in advance; getting to them can cost as much as $350 per flight hour. The refuge's staff answers hundreds of letters each year from people wanting to see bears and who have no idea that the refuge is a place of wilderness, with no developed trails, roads or campgrounds. Those who come into the refuge visitor center in Kodiak all have one question: "Where can we see bears?"

Chances of encountering a bear on Kodiak are as good as anywhere in the world; there are nearly 3,000 bears here, about a bear to every square mile to mile-and-a-half, a density rivaled only by Admiralty Island in southeastern Alaska and Katmai National Park on the Alaska Peninsula.

To accommodate the public's fascination with bears and to control the impacts of unrestricted visitation, the Kodiak National Wildlife Refuge launched a bear-viewing program in the early 1990s. It operated in 1990 and 1991 at Dog Salmon Creek off Fraser Lake near Olga Bay, and was moved in 1992 to a site of thick bear concentrations at O'Malley River off Karluk Lake. More than 260 people from around the world applied

These browns scuffle at the upper falls on Dog Salmon Creek. The refuge's bear-viewing program operated two years on this creek, adjacent to a fish counting weir. One reason the program was moved was because participants said the sight of bears next to and climbing on the weir decreased the wilderness experience. (David Menke)

for the program's 90 permits in 1992. Groups of six people visited the camp for four-day stretches from July to mid-

September, where they spent the days on a wooden pad watching up to 40 bears at a time. The premise behind the program, patterned after a similar one operated by the state at McNeil River on the Alaska Peninsula, is that bears and people can coexist as long as people follow a predictable pattern.

Bear populations on Kodiak are as healthy and stable as they have ever been, largely because of government protection. The Kodiak National Wildlife Refuge serves as a bear sanctuary on Kodiak, Afognak, Ban and Uganik islands, covering 1.6 million acres, excluding inholdings, about 60 percent of

KODIAK NATIONAL WILDLIFE REFUGE

Kodiak National Wildlife Refuge (shaded area) takes in 1.6 million acres on Kodiak and neighboring islands. Private inholdings within the refuge are not shown on the map. As of mid-1992, these inholdings totaled 300,000 acres, mostly in small parcels.
(*Source:* U.S. Fish & Wildlife Service; *ALASKA GEOGRAPHIC*® map by Kathy Doogan)

the total brown bear habitat in the archipelago. Most of the habitat is undeveloped and pristine, and bear hunting is tightly controlled by the state to avoid depleting populations.

But some are less than thrilled that Kodiak bears are thriving. Rancher Omar Stratman says bears have been killing his cattle for years, and now they are getting more brazen about it. In 1992, a brown bear attacked a cow in the corral outside Stratman's house. Bears are seen more frequently around town these days, causing commotion wherever they go. In 1992, there were reports of bears in the Pizza Hut parking lot, outside some homes on the Coast Guard base, even peering into the window at the Buskin River Inn. The remote villages know bears well. In Larsen Bay, where salmon-rich Humpy Creek passes through the middle of town, bear claw-marks adorn the outside of more than one home, and parents routinely summon their children inside during "bear time" of summer evenings when bears come to feed at the creek. Some folks blame the "Bear Farm," as they unflatteringly call the refuge, for protecting bears to the point that they are overrunning peopled places.

Refuge bear biologist Vic Barnes and Roger Smith, area wildlife biologist with the Alaska Department of Fish and Game for the last 20 years, are used to hearing such criticism. "Actually it is amazing that we have so many bears and so few incidents," says Barnes. Yet wildlife managers worry about increasing conflicts between people and bears. Bears are opportunistic feeders, attracted by unclean hunting and fishing camps and remote garbage dumps. Kodiak's

rising popularity with deer hunters and sport fishermen coincides with an increase with problem bears during the last decade. Some villages are trying to reduce bear visits by fencing landfills and one village is going to incinerate garbage. Outside hunting season, bears may be killed only in "defense of life or property." The DLP kill is relatively small — 7.2 bears a year from 1974 to 1986 compared to an average of 147 bears killed during the annual sport harvest — but DLPs tend to be concentrated near villages and hunting areas and could reduce populations locally.

On a wider scale, future development and occupation of private lands within the refuge could produce chronic bear problems and destroy prime bear habitat, say bear biologists. About 330,000 acres within the refuge are private lands, most acquired by Kodiak's Native corporations through passage of the Alaska Native Claims Settlement Act of 1971. Many of these inholdings encompass world-class bear habitat, including part of Karluk Lake and River.

ABOUT THE KODIAK BEARS

Kodiak browns live on the largest islands of the Kodiak archipelago. Kodiak and Afognak islands provide about 92 percent of the bear habitat in the archipelago while Shuyak, Raspberry, Uganik, Sitkalidak, Ban and several smaller islands make up the remainder. The range of these uniquely large animals is relatively small, attesting to the rich food sources available to them.

Kodiak bears grow to be among the largest land carnivores in the world, rivaled only by polar bears. The largest Kodiak male bears may weigh up to 1,500 pounds and stand nearly 10 feet tall. Their claws may reach 3.5 inches along the curve, turning an ivory color on older animals. The oldest boar known from Kodiak was 24 years old, and the oldest sow was 35. Of the top 50 trophy bears listed by Boone and Crockett, 33 came from the Kodiak archipelago.

These island bears comprise a distinct subspecies of the brown/grizzly bears found elsewhere in North America. Besides being the biggest brown bears, they have distinct cranial characteristics with exceptionally wide cheekbones. These bears are physically isolated by the Gulf of Alaska and Shelikof Strait from other brown bear/grizzly populations on the Alaska mainland. (Mammal taxonomists consider brown and grizzly bears of North America, Europe and Asia to be the same species, *Ursus arctos*. The term "brown bear" is normally used to describe brown bears of coastal regions that generally are larger, because of diets that include an abundance of fish, than the "grizzly bears" of inland areas. The grizzly is considered a "threatened" species in the Lower 48.) Kodiak bears are designated *Ursus arctos middendorffi*, while browns/ grizzlies through the rest of North America are labeled *Ursus arctos horribilis*.

The bears of Kodiak emerge from their winter dens from March through June. Adult males and single adult females are the first out, followed by females with yearlings or older juveniles, young adults and females with cubs. The cubs, born in January and February in the dens, are nearly hairless at birth but quickly grow fur that may be four inches long by fall. They often have a white collar that fades to blond or brown by the spring of their second year. Female Kodiak

This adolescent bear scampers through a creek in search of dinner (above left) and comes up with a sockeye salmon. Salmon begin turning red when they leave salt water and enter fresh water to spawn. (Both by Don Pitcher)

browns are most productive between ages 9 and 16, and have litters of one to three cubs about every third or fourth year.

As the hungry bears leave their dens in the higher elevations, they forage mountain slopes for emerging forbs, sedges and grasses. Some descend to near sea level to feed on herbaceous plants and carrion. The arrival of salmon to streams and lakes abruptly alters their dining habits. Key areas where bears congregate include the Ayakulik/Red, Sturgeon, Karluk, O'Malley, Little and Terror rivers, Dog Salmon and Humpy creeks, the tributaries and shores of Karluk, Red and Upper Station lakes, and streams at the heads of Uyak, Deadman and Sulua bays. Bears feed on salmon as long as the fish are available, which may be mid-June to mid-December depending on the area. During a brief period in July and early August, bears also congregate in alpine areas in the central and northern portions of the refuge to eat nutrient-rich sedges and forbs uncovered by receding snow.

Bears apparently crave elderberries. They begin foraging on the berry bushes in early August, before the crop even ripens. They also feed on salmonberry, lowbush cranberry, bearberry, crowberry and devil's club, with a particular fondness for highbush cranberry.

By mid-November, most bears in the northern part of the refuge are entering their dens. Those in the southern region den two to three weeks later.

Bears in the wild face two-legged predators twice a year. The state allows a spring hunt from April 1 to May 15 and a fall hunt from October 25 to November 30. In addition to seasons, hunting is regulated by permits and bag limits. Sport hunters

Bear-viewing on Kodiak now centers around O'Malley River, which drains into Karluk Lake, where this sow and cubs were photographed. (Marion Stirrup)

consider pelts taken in late fall to be the best quality, because the hair is denser and darker. These hunts are for trophy bears, the largest males. All nonresident hunters must be accompanied by a state-licensed bear guide. About 25 to 30 bear guides work the Kodiak area, according to ADF&G's Smith.

Compared to sport hunting, which in 1989 accounted for 151 bear kills, few Kodiak bears have historically been killed for food. Currently there is no subsistence bear hunting on Kodiak although in 1992 the federal subsistence board was considering subsistence bear hunts for villages that can show traditional and customary use of bears as food.

ABOUT THE REFUGE

The love-hate relationship between the humans and bears of Kodiak reaches years back. Fishermen and ranchers viewed bears as unfriendly competitors. Wanton killing of bears was common in the early 1900s, and commercial hunts were not regulated until 1925. A major complaint lodged by ranchers in the late 1930s resulted in field investigations by the Alaska Game Commission, and agents dispatched 11 bears. But cattle losses blamed on bears were greatly exaggerated, according to one investigator, who attributed only five of 79 cattle deaths to bears, the rest from malnutrition, plant poisonings, falls and drownings.

About this time, hunters and conservationists became concerned about the welfare of the Kodiak bear and from their efforts came creation of Kodiak National Wildlife Refuge, on Aug. 19, 1941.

The refuge initially occupied about 1,957,000 acres, which included much of Kodiak and all of Uganik islands. A one-mile strip around the coast of Kodiak Island remained outside refuge borders to accommodate homesteading, commercial fishing camps and canneries. In 1951, the newly formed Kodiak Stock Growers Association asked the territorial legislature to remove protection from bears. The house passed a 12-month open season on bears with no bag limit, action supported by the Kodiak Chamber of Commerce. But because bear guiding was lucrative, the guides asked the Alaska Game Commission to not enact such a liberal hunt. The proposal to eliminate bears drew national attention. In *Audubon* magazine, writer I.N. Gabrielson opined: "If it comes to a choice between killing off the bears and trying to develop the optimistically estimated herd of 3,800 range cattle, it is my belief that this country ought to set aside the entire island to preserve the splendid Kodiak bears."

During the next decade, the Bureau of Land Management, which managed grazing leases, and the U.S. Fish and Wildlife Service, which managed the bears, tried to resolve the problems. In 1958, Kupreanoff and Shearwater peninsulas were removed from the refuge to add grazing land for expansion of the cattle industry, eight square-mile Native village sites were deleted, and the one-mile coastal strip was added. Conflicts continued. High bear harvests in the mid-1960s brought about hunting restrictions.

Then from 1964 to 1968, the Alaska Department of Fish and Game conducted a controversial bear control program to help ranchers. The department employed a former World War II pilot to shoot bears from the air. He mounted a .30 caliber M-1 semiautomatic rifle on top of his Piper plane so it shot above the propeller, fired by remote trigger. Operating in as much secrecy as possible, the pilot randomly shot 35 bears, whether or not they were responsible for cattle killing. Bear guides, enraged over the slaughter, got pictures published of the plane and the resulting outcry ended the operation. After that, the department considered various other solutions, and even bought fencing to enclose grazing leases but never erected it.

In 1971, about 330,000 acres including some of the archipelago's most productive fish and wildlife habitats transferred into Native ownership. Passage in 1980 of the Alaska National Interest Lands Conservation Act added about 50,000 acres on Afognak and Ban islands to the refuge.

During the 1970s and 1980s, attention focused on construction of the Terror Lake Hydroelectric Project, about 25 miles southwest of the City of Kodiak. About a third of the project area was located within the refuge. Concerns about impacts on fish and wildlife, particularly brown bears, resulted in use of an oil-fired garbage incinerator, prohibition of firearms, frequent

bear safety lectures to workers, a government environmental monitor on site, and creation of the Kodiak Brown Bear Research and Habitat Maintenance Trust. Although more than 400 workers occupied the project site, only one bear was killed and apparently the construction had no adverse affects on the bears, based on a five-year study of about 50 bears that wore radio-collars so their movements could be monitored. Some residents in nearby Port Lions complained that the activity drove more bears than usual into town, a claim disputed by biologists who told residents at a public meeting that failed berry crops and depleted salmon runs

were the reasons more bears were feeding at their landfill.

What is the future of Kodiak browns? That apparently depends in part on what happens to the private inholdings, say refuge managers.

The Native corporations, as set out by ANCSA, were to use their holdings to return profits to their shareholders. For the past eight years, Native leaders have quietly sought congressional approval for a cash

These Kodiak browns rest from a busy round of fishing. (Don Pitcher)

buy-out or land swap of their property in the refuge's interior, but their appeal was lost in discussions over oil drilling on the coastal plain of the Arctic National Wildlife Refuge. In 1992, Akhiok-Kaguyak and Old Harbor village corporations mounted a massive media campaign, hired a Washington D.C.-based public relations man, and all summer hosted tours of their land for dozens of journalists, environmentalists and congressional staffers. The Natives are far from getting the deal they want — about $1,000 an acre for about 317,000 acres.

Native corporations plan to develop their lands with wilderness lodges, cabins and camps. Akhiok-Kaguyak even applied for a

The O'Malley River drainage supports perhaps as many as 90 bears during summer and fall salmon runs. Visitors to the Kodiak National Wildlife Refuge bear-viewing program at O'Malley might see as many as 40 bears at the peak salmon runs, but gatherings of 15 to 20 bears at a time are more typical. (David Menke)

Department of Energy grant to study using their land as a temporary nuclear waste dump. Refuge managers fear any development that concentrates people in bear-rich areas could ultimately end in disaster. Although guides and outfitters are limited on refuge lands, those restrictions may not extend to private inholdings. Although the law says that private inholdings must be used in a way compatible with the purposes of the refuge, the true legal meaning of this provision are unclear and have not been tested in court. The outlook for these lands and the bears that depend on them remains uncertain and troubling.

In the meantime, refuge managers are determining the future of the bear-viewing program at O'Malley River. Among other things, they will decide whether it can be turned over to a private company to operate, said George Constantino, regional supervisor for refuges with the U.S. Fish and Wildlife Service in Anchorage. People with guiding, sightseeing and wildlife viewing companies on Kodiak are worried about government-funded competition and would like to see the program offered as a concession, he said. The program is expensive for the refuge to operate, so contracting it out will be considered. Some costs in starting the O'Malley River program included erecting sleeping and cooking quarters, purchasing radio equipment, and paying salaries and some overtime to two on-site rangers, said Paul Taylor, program administrator in Kodiak. "Concession-operated visitor facilities can be done well," Taylor said. "It depends on how well the agreements are written and how closely the concessionaires are monitored."

The viewing program coincides with

ongoing study of bear-people interactions. For two years, researchers have camped on a distant hill to observe bear-people encounters in the O'Malley River drainage. During the first year, when people visited independently and stayed in the public use cabin or camped, researchers saw enough random disturbances to make bears quit using the area. They also documented the death of one cub directly related to people fishing and watching bears; two cubs got separated from the sow in the tall grass and ran into a boar that killed one of them. In 1992, researchers again watched the drainage to see how controlled visitation affected the bears, and whether the program succeeded in providing safe bear-viewing with minimal impact on the animals.

At the same time, some bear guides apparently fear that the bear-viewing program could become so popular that bear hunting will be halted in that part of the refuge. Constantino said that while a public outcry against hunting is always possible, there are no plans to discontinue bear hunts. He said the bears that become most habituated to people are those with cubs; sows are rarely hunted and only when they are without cubs, every three or four years. The big boars, which are sought by hunters, are wary and appear on the fringes of the viewing area. "We think we can craft a program to continue the traditional activities, which draw a large clientele, and also start new programs that attract a different group," Constantino said. Inquiries about the bear-viewing program should be made to the Kodiak National Wildlife Refuge Visitor's Center, 1390 Buskin River Road, Kodiak, Alaska 99615.

Bibliography

A Description of the Social and Economic Systems of the Kodiak/Shumagin Region. Minerals Management Service Technical Report 122. Anchorage: Cultural Dynamics, Ltd., 1986.

A Sociocultural Description of Small Communities in the Kodiak/Shumagin Region. Mineral Management Service Technical Report 121. Anchorage: Cultural Dynamics Ltd., 1986.

Adasiak, Allan. "Moonrise in Kodiak: The Unification Church Goes Fishing," *The Alaska Journal.* Anchorage: Alaska Northwest Publishing Co., Vol. 10, No. 1, Winter 1980.

Alaska Geographic Society. *Kodiak, Island of Change,* Anchorage: Alaska Northwest Publishing Co., 1977.

Alekseev, A.I. *The Destiny of Russian America 1741-1867.* Translated by Marina Ramsay, edited by R.A. Pierce. Kingston, Ontario and Fairbanks Alaska: The Limestone Press, 1990.

Analysis of Program Options and Priorities. The Kodiak Brown Bear Research and Habitat Maintenance Trust. Anchorage: The LTN Group, 1992.

Balzar, John. "Laws Clash in Kodiak Wilderness," *The Los Angeles Times.* Los Angeles: Times Mirror Co. Sept. 12, 1991.

Black, Lydia. *The Russian Conquest of Kodiak.* Anthropological Papers of the University of Alaska. Fairbanks, In Press.

Buck, Eugene H., William J. Wilson, Larry S. Lau, Caedmon Liburd and Harold W. Searby. *Kadyak, a Background for Living.* Anchorage: Arctic Environmental Information and Data Center, University of Alaska, 1975.

Chaffin, Yule. *Koniag to King Crab.* Chaffin Incorporated, 1967.

_____ *Alaska's Konyag Country.* 1983.

Clark, Donald W. "Koniag Prehistory". *Tubinger Monographien zur Urgeschicte,* Band 1. Stuttgart: Verlag W. Kohlhammer, 1974.

_____. "Ocean Bay: An Early North Pacific Maritime Culture." *Archaeological Survey of Canada,* Paper No. 86. National Museum of Man, Mercury Series. Ottawa, 1979.

Cloe, John Haile. *The Aleutian Warriors, a History of the 11th Air Force & Fleet Air Wing 4, Part 1.* Anchorage Chapter, Air Force Association and Pictorial Histories Publishing Co., Inc., Missoula: 1991.

Colonial Russian America, Kyrill T. Khlebnikov's Reports, 1817-1832. Translated by Basil Dmytryshyn and E.A.P. Crownhart-Vaughan. Portland: Oregon Historical Society, 1976.

"Community Profiles Developed for the Social Impact Assessment of the Inshore/Offshore Amendment Proposal." North Pacific Fisheries Management Council. LaJolla, Calif: Impact Assessment, Inc., January 1991.

Davydov, G.I. *Two Voyages to Russian America, 1802-1807.* Edited by Richard A. Pierce. Translated by Colin Bearne. Kingston, Ontario: The Limestone Press, 1977.

de Laguna, Frederica. *The Archaeology of Cook Inlet, Alaska.* Philadelphia: University of Pennsylvania Press, 1934.

Fitzhugh, William W. and Aron Crowell. *Crossroads of Continents: Cultures of Siberia and Alaska.* Washington, D.C.: Smithsonian Institution Press, 1988.

Griggs, Robert F. *The Valley of Ten Thousand Smokes.* Washington: The National Geographic Society, 1922.

Haggarty, James C., Christopher B. Wooley, Jon M. Erlandson and Aron Crowell. *The 1990 Exxon Cultural Resource Program, Site Protection and Maritime Cultural Ecology in Prince William Sound and the Gulf of Alaska.* Anchorage: Exxon Shipping Co. and Exxon Company USA, 1991.

Harvey, Lola. *Derevnia's Daughters, Saga of an Alaskan Village.* Manhattan, Kansas: Sunflower University Press, 1991.

Heizer, Robert. "Archaeology of the Uyak Site, Kodiak Island, Alaska." *University of California, Anthropological Records.* Vol. 17(1). Berkeley: University of California Press, 1956.

Huggins, Eli Lundy. *Kodiak and Afognak Life, 1868-1870.* Edited by Richard A. Pierce. Kingston, Ontario, Canada: The Limestone Press, 1981.

Kaplan, David. "Born Free, Sold Dear: America's premier bear refuge is up for bids because native Alaskans have run out of money." *Newsweek.* May 6, 1991.

Khlebnikov, K.T. *Baranov, Chief Manager of the Russian Colonies in America.* Translated by Colin Bearne, edited by Richard A. Pierce. Kingston, Ontario: The Limestone Press, 1973.

Kodiak National Wildlife Refuge Final Comprehensive Conservation Plan, Wilderness Review and Environmental Impact Statement. Anchorage: U.S. Fish and Wildlife Service, 1987.

Kodiak Tsunami, First 29 Days, City of Kodiak, 1964.

Lisiansky, Urey. *Voyage Round the World in the Years 1803, 1804, 1805 and 1806.* Ridgewood, N.J: The Gregg Press, 1968.

McCloskey, William B. Jr. *Highliners.* New York: McGraw-Hill Book Co., 1979.

Pierce, Richard A., ed. *The Round the World Voyage of Hieromonk Gideon, 1803-1809.* Translated with introduction and notes by Lydia T. Black. Kingston, Ontario and Fairbanks, Alaska: The Limestone Press and University of Alaska, 1989.

Rostad, Michael. *Time to Dance: Life of an Alaska Native.* Anchorage: A.T. Publishing Inc., 1988.

Roppel, Patricia. *Salmon from Kodiak, a History of the Salmon Fishery of Kodiak Island, Alaska.* Anchorage: Alaska Historical Commission, 1986.

Sarber, Hosea R. *Report of the Kodiak Brown Bear Control Project.* Alaska Game Commission, 1939.

Sharpsteen, Bill. "Native Claims: Native Alaskans, by Congressional Decree, Manage Their Fate Through Native-Owned Corporations — But Turning a Profit May Cost Wilderness." *Buzzworm: The Environmental Journal.* Vol. IV, No. 3, May/June 1992, pp. 44-49.

Smith, Roger, Victor G. Barnes Jr. and Lawrence J. Van Daele. "Brown Bear-Human Conflicts in the Kodiak Archipelago, Alaska." From symposium on bear management strategies, Northwest Territories Dept. of Renewable Resources, 1989.

Tikhmenev, P.A. *A History of the Russian-American Company.* Translated and edited by Richard A. Pierce and Alton S. Donnelly. Seattle: University of Washington Press, 1978.

Troyer, Willard A. and Richard J. Hensel. *The Brown Bear of Kodiak Island.* U.S. Dept. of Interior, Fish and Wildlife Service, Bureau of Sport Fisheries and Wildlife, Division of Refuges. Anchorage, 1969.

Index

ALASKA GEOGRAPHIC® back issues

The North Slope, Vol. 1, No. 1. Charter issue. Out of print.

One Man's Wilderness, Vol. 1, No. 2. Out of print.

Admiralty…Island in Contention, Vol. 1, No. 3. $7.50.

Fisheries of the North Pacific, Vol. 1, No. 4. Out of print.

The Alaska-Yukon Wild Flowers Guide, Vol. 2, No. 1. Out of print.

Richard Harrington's Yukon, Vol. 2, No. 2. Out of print.

Prince William Sound, Vol. 2, No. 3. Out of print.

Yakutat: The Turbulent Crescent, Vol. 2, No. 4. Out of print.

Glacier Bay: Old Ice, New Land, Vol. 3, No. 1. Out of print.

The Land: Eye of the Storm, Vol. 3, No. 2. Out of print.

Richard Harrington's Antarctic, Vol. 3, No. 3. $12.95.

The Silver Years of the Alaska Canned Salmon Industry: An Album of Historical Photos, Vol. 3, No. 4. $17.95.

Alaska's Volcanoes: Northern Link In the Ring of Fire, Vol. 4, No. 1. Out of print.

The Brooks Range, Vol. 4, No. 2. Out of print.

Kodiak: Island of Change, Vol. 4, No. 3. Out of print.

Wilderness Proposals, Vol. 4, No. 4. Out of print.

Cook Inlet Country, Vol. 5, No. 1. Out of print.

Southeast: Alaska's Panhandle, Vol. 5, No. 2. Out of print.

Bristol Bay Basin, Vol. 5, No. 3. Out of print.

Alaska Whales and Whaling, Vol. 5, No. 4. $19.95.

Yukon-Kuskokwim Delta, Vol. 6, No. 1. Out of print.

Aurora Borealis, Vol. 6, No. 2. $14.95.

Alaska's Native People, Vol. 6, No. 3. $24.95.

The Stikine River, Vol. 6, No. 4. $12.95.

Alaska's Great Interior, Vol. 7, No. 1. $17.95.

A Photographic Geography of Alaska, Vol. 7, No. 2. $17.95.

The Aleutians, Vol. 7, No. 3. $19.95.

Klondike Lost: A Decade of Photographs by Kinsey & Kinsey, Vol. 7, No. 4. Out of print.

Wrangell-Saint Elias, Vol. 8, No. 1. $19.95.

Alaska Mammals, Vol. 8, No. 2. $15.95.

The Kotzebue Basin, Vol. 8, No. 3. $15.95.

Alaska National Interest Lands, Vol. 8, No. 4. $17.95.

Alaska's Glaciers, Vol. 9, No. 1. Out of print.

Sitka and Its Ocean/Island World, Vol. 9, No. 2. $19.95.

Islands of the Seals: The Pribilofs, Vol. 9, No. 3. $12.95.

Alaska's Oil/Gas & Minerals Industry, Vol. 9, No. 4. $15.95.

Adventure Roads North, Vol. 10, No. 1. $17.95.

Anchorage and the Cook Inlet Basin, Vol. 10, No. 2. $17.95.

Alaska's Salmon Fisheries, Vol. 10, No. 3. $15.95.

Up the Koyukuk, Vol. 10, No. 4. $17.95.

Nome: City of the Golden Beaches, Vol. 11, No. 1. $14.95.

Alaska's Farms and Gardens, Vol. 11, No. 2. $15.95.

Chilkat River Valley, Vol. 11, No. 3. $15.95.

Alaska Steam, Vol. 11, No. 4. $14.95.

Northwest Territories, Vol. 12, No. 1. $17.95.

Alaska's Forest Resources, Vol. 12, No. 2. $16.95.

Alaska Native Arts and Crafts, Vol. 12, No. 3. $17.95.

Our Arctic Year, Vol. 12, No. 4. $15.95.

Where Mountains Meet the Sea: Alaska's Gulf Coast, Vol. 13, No. 1. $17.95.

Backcountry Alaska, Vol. 13, No. 2. $17.95.

British Columbia's Coast, Vol. 13, No. 3. $17.95.

Lake Clark/Lake Iliamna Country, Vol. 13, No. 4. Out of print.

Dogs of the North, Vol. 14, No. 1. $17.95.

South/Southeast Alaska, Vol. 14, No. 2. Out of print.

Alaska's Seward Peninsula, Vol. 14, No. 3. $15.95.

The Upper Yukon Basin, Vol. 14, No. 4. $17.95.

Glacier Bay: Icy Wilderness, Vol. 15, No. 1. Out of print.

Dawson City, Vol. 15, No. 2. $15.95.

Denali, Vol. 15, No. 3. $16.95.

The Kuskokwim River, Vol. 15, No. 4. $17.95.

Katmai Country, Vol. 16, No. 1. $17.95.

North Slope Now, Vol. 16, No. 2. $14.95.

The Tanana Basin, Vol. 16, No. 3. $17.95.

The Copper Trail, Vol. 16, No. 4. $17.95.

The Nushagak Basin, Vol. 17, No. 1. $17.95.

Juneau, Vol. 17, No. 2. $17.95.

The Middle Yukon River, Vol. 17, No. 3. $17.95.

The Lower Yukon River, Vol. 17, No. 4. $17.95.

Alaska's Weather, Vol. 18, No. 1. $17.95.

Alaska's Volcanoes, Vol. 18, No. 2. $17.95.

Admiralty Island: Fortress of the Bears, Vol. 18, No. 3. $17.95.

Unalaska/Dutch Harbor, Vol. 18, No. 4. $17.95.

Skagway: A Legacy of Gold, Vol. 19, No. 1. $18.95.

ALASKA: The Great Land, Vol. 19, No. 2. $18.95.

ALL PRICES SUBJECT TO CHANGE.

Your $39 membership in The Alaska Geographic Society includes four subsequent issues of *ALASKA GEOGRAPHIC*®, the Society's official quarterly. Please add $10 for non-U.S. memberships.

Additional membership information is available upon request. Single copies of the *ALASKA GEOGRAPHIC*® back issues are also available. When ordering, please make payments in U.S. funds and add $2.00 postage/handling per copy book rate; $4.00 per copy for Priority mail. Non-U.S. postage extra. Free catalog available. To order back issues send your check or money order and volumes desired to:

The Alaska Geographic Society

P.O. Box 93370
Anchorage, AK 99509

NEXT ISSUE: *Alaska's Railroads*, Vol. 19, No. 4. Before there were roads, rivers and railroads provided the main arteries for Alaska's commerce. This issue will look at the various lines that contributed to Alaska's railroad history, and assess their economic impact on the state. To members, 1992, with index $18.95.

ALASKA'S ALIEN ANIMALS

BY EDGAR P. BAILEY

Editor's note: *A biologist with the U.S. Fish and Wildlife Service's Alaska Maritime National Wildlife Refuge, Ed has spent many years exploring the Aleutians and Alaska's other islands.*

Most people believe that Alaska islands are largely undisturbed by modern civilization, especially when compared to the majority of the world's temperate and tropical islands, nearly all of which have been seriously affected by introduced plants and animals and other human activities. Although hundreds of Alaska islands are currently still uninhabited by humans, few islands escaped the drastic ecological changes caused by the introduction of foxes, ground squirrels, rats, cattle and other alien animals. Game animals, such as deer, elk and bison, have also been introduced to many islands and to Alaska's mainland.

FOXES

In 1750, only nine years after Vitus Bering landed on Kayak Island in the Gulf of Alaska and on the Shumagin Islands south of the Alaska Peninsula, the first Russian

settlers brought arctic foxes from the Commander Islands in Russia and released them on Attu, westernmost of the Aleutian Islands. Numerous other islands in the Aleutians that had no native land mammals soon were stocked with arctic and red foxes for fur trapping. Aleut midden sites revealed no terrestrial mammal bones before the arrival of the Russians, thus confirming that the Aleutian chain west of at least

Umnak Island was devoid of foxes and all other land mammals at the end of Pleistocene glaciations, approximately 10,000 years ago. Interisland passes west of Umnak remained below sea level, and thus prevented mammals inhabiting the Alaska or Siberian mainland from colonizing the central and western Aleutians. During glacial periods red foxes reached Unimak, Unalaska, Umnak and other islands in the eastern Aleutians,

By far the greatest number of fox farms were made up of arctic foxes. As early as 1750, the Russians imported arctic foxes from the Commander Islands to Attu Island, westernmost of the Aleutians. During the peak of the fox farming industry in the early 1900s, the U.S. government had leased nearly 400 Alaska islands to fox farmers, who raised 36,000 foxes with a value of about $6 million. The industry collapsed in the 1930s, and was dead by World War II. (Jo Overholt)

which the early Russian explorers aptly named the Fox Islands. Foxes and certain other small mammals also naturally reached Kodiak and many other islands south of the Alaska Peninsula and in the Gulf of Alaska by way of ice or land bridges. Foxes are indigenous to virtually all islands in the Bering Sea and Arctic Ocean because they are accessible in winter on pack ice.

Although no documentation exists, it is also possible that Aleuts or other Alaska Natives may have transported small animals to islands on which they were not indigenous. However, this is unlikely in the case of foxes because archaeological evidence reveals that prior to the arrival of the promyshlenniki, the Russian fur traders, the Aleuts apparently

Most of the introduced red foxes used in the fox farming industry came from Unimak, Unalaska or other large islands in the eastern Aleutians or from the Alaska Peninsula. Foxes migrated to these islands over ice during the Pleistocene glaciation, which ended about 10,000 years ago. (Roy M. Corral)

made little use of foxes. The Native people on Kodiak, on the other hand, used foxes for furs and pets. As settlement of Alaska by Russians and later by Americans progressed, additional species were introduced both deliberately and accidentally on hundreds of Alaska islands and eventually in various areas of the mainland .

The main impetus for American fox farming originated about 1880 on Prince William Island, located off the Atlantic coast of Canada, and then spread across the continent to Alaska. The introduction of silver foxes, a dark phase of the red fox, on one of the Shumagin Islands in the 1880s was believed the beginning of fox farming by Americans in Alaska.

By far the most profound changes brought about by introduced species were on islands because of their biological isolation. Many species of birds evolved nesting on islands free of terrestrial predators, and thus lacked defenses for survival when predators like foxes appeared. Unequivocally, the advent of island fox farming, which peaked in the 1930s, was the worst ecological catastrophe experienced in Alaska. Between 1750 and World War II, which ended the insular fox farming era, foxes had been released on more than 450 islands from the Alexander Archipelago in southeastern Alaska to the western end of the Aleutians. Most arctic foxes released on islands originated from the Commander Islands or the Pribilofs, but some were obtained from as far away as Greenland. Most introduced red foxes came from Unimak, Unalaska or other large islands in the eastern Aleutians or from the Alaska Peninsula, but some reportedly came from Kamchatka in Russia.

The U.S. government began leasing Alaska islands for the propagation of foxes in 1882, and by 1900 at least 32 islands were under lease. Fox farming grew rapidly in the early 1900s, especially after the protection of sea otters and fur seals. By 1925 with increasing demand for fox furs because of fashion trends, the number of islands leased for fox farming rose to nearly 400 with 36,000 foxes valued at about $6 million. In 1928, fur production was the third largest industry in Alaska, surpassed only by fishing and mining. In 1929, the peak year, 9,300 arctic fox pelts valued at about $900,000 were exported from Alaska. In the Aleutians alone, approximately 27,000 fox pelts were taken between 1913 and 1936. At the industry's zenith in the early 1900s outlandish prices were reported: Individual pelts of silver foxes sold for as high as $2,800 in London and prime breeding pairs for $34,000. Prime arctic or blue fox pelts sometimes sold for more than $150.

Forty percent of island fox farms were in southeastern Alaska (182), followed by the Aleutian Islands (86), Prince William Sound and other islands in the Gulf of Alaska (73), islands south of the Alaska Peninsula (63), and lastly the Kodiak archipelago where foxes were reportedly released on at least 51 islands. In all areas the vast majority of islands were stocked with arctic foxes. Island fox farms drastically declined in the 1930s after the onset of the Great Depression. By 1931 the price of arctic fox pelts from the Aleutians declined from an average of $108 two years earlier to only $32. Attempts to revive island fox farming after World War II failed.

Throughout the world predation by exotic species on islands has been primarily responsible for the decline or extinction of more seabird populations than any other factor, and Alaska islands are no different. The adverse effects of introduced foxes became known earliest in the Aleutians. As early as 1811, about 20 years after arctic foxes were introduced on Atka Island, local Aleuts were complaining that foxes were driving away birds that formerly were numerous and whose feathers and skins were used for clothing. Likewise, on Attu Island and elsewhere Aleuts were having to go to other islands to secure birds or were forced to use fish skins for clothing. In 1874 William Dall, one of the earliest naturalists in Alaska, portrayed the marked differences in bird life on islands with alien foxes compared to those still free of introduced predators. But not until the 1930s when Olaus Murie documented the vanishing waterfowl and seabirds in the Aleutians did government policy gradually shift from facilitating insular fox farming to concern for saving some islands for nesting birds. Fox trappers deliberately chose the best bird islands to release foxes on because they regarded birds merely as fox food. On island after island nesting puffins, auklets, storm-petrels, eiders, Aleutian Canada geese, ptarmigan and other birds disappeared because of introduced foxes. By 1950, Aleutian Canada geese were thought to survive on only one small island in their former range that extended from the Kurile Islands north of Japan across the Aleutians to small fox-free islands around Kodiak Island. In 1979 and 1982 relict populations of this endangered species were found nesting on two other small islands.

The havoc wreaked on islands on which foxes were liberated can be illustrated by a few cases where the loss of birds was quantified. For example, a dozen red foxes on a 1,500-acre island off Newfoundland in Canada killed an estimated 31,000 seabirds in a single breeding season. This is approximately the same number of birds that were picked up along beaches after the *Exxon Valdez* oil spill. In 1976 two red foxes reached Shaiak Island in Bristol Bay, site of 156,000 nesting seabirds, and severely reduced the nesting

success of seven species of seabirds. Most of the 50,000 murres nesting on the island's sod slopes lost their eggs, and all common eiders lost their nests to foxes. Foxes kill far more birds than their immediate needs because they cache birds and eggs for later use when breeding birds have migrated for the winter. The degree of devastation of colonial nesting seabirds caused by introduced predators elsewhere in the world can perhaps be most graphically illustrated on Kerguelen Island in the southern Indian Ocean where an estimated

1,200,000 seabirds a year were being killed by feral cats, a figure far greater than the total bird mortality caused by the Exxon spill. Besides devastating bird colonies, on some islands foxes ultimately cause pronounced changes in island vegetation because of the lack of recycled excrement from thousands of birds to enrich soils.

Fortunately alien foxes only presently remain on 46 islands in Alaska. In southeastern Alaska and Prince William Sound both red and arctic foxes were removed by

trappers prior to abandoning their islands or they died out naturally. Unlike on tundra-covered islands south of the Alaska Peninsula and in the Aleutians where foxes continued to thrive on many islands after fox farmers left, the animals are not well suited to

Severe overgrazing by ground squirrels and voles has led to erosion on Chankluit Island south of the Alaska Peninsula. Introduced cattle, reindeer, caribou and other grazers have damaged habitat on many Alaska islands. (Nina Faust)

islands covered by rain forest. Foxes disappeared on nearly all islands lacking good beaches for scavenging and foraging for intertidal invertebrates after they eliminated most nesting seabirds, waterfowl and shorebirds. Fox farmers

Arctic ground squirrels have considerably harmed some habitats. Russians and early American fox farmers released squirrels and other rodents on islands with fox farms to provide additional food for the foxes. (Roy M. Corral)

generally regarded seabird islands as good for only so long, in other words, only while the birds lasted.

The U.S. Fish and Wildlife Service began removing foxes from Amchitka Island, now part of the Aleutians Island Unit of Alaska Maritime National Wildlife Refuge and then part of the Aleutian Islands National Wildlife Refuge in 1949, but they have been eradicated from only 21 islands to date largely because the use of poisons, the most effective means of eliminating foxes, has been

banned. Moreover, less than 1 percent of the refuge's budget is devoted to eradicating foxes, the activity that benefits island birds the most. The little ongoing fox removal activity relies on the use of traps, but it will not be possible to eliminate all foxes from large islands without poisons, which can be employed safely in the Aleutians since no non-target land mammals are native to most of the region.

After the removal of alien foxes from several islands in the Aleutians, dramatic recoveries in bird populations have been documented. Aleutian Canada geese are once again nesting on several islands where they were extirpated by foxes, and phenomenal increases in seabirds are occurring. On one small island in the western Aleutians, for example, 24 species of breeding birds increased substantially within seven years after foxes were gone, and 12 species of seabirds rose more than 500 percent. In 14 years cormorants increased from about 20 individuals to 650. An island in the eastern Aleutians that Olaus Murie recommended to continue as a fox farm nearly 60 years ago because foxes had eliminated nearly all the birds now has more than 125,000 nesting seabirds. Unfortunately certain extirpated species like ptarmigan on some islands may not be able to recolonize their former habitat for a long period.

RODENTS

After alien foxes the most severe

ecological impacts on Alaska islands have been wrought by introduced rodents, especially rats. The first known introduction of rats occurred when a Japanese ship ran aground in 1780 on an island in the central Aleutians later named Rat Island by the Russians. In many cases the release of ground squirrels, voles and other rodents was directly attributed to fox farming. In the early 1800s the Russian American Co. encouraged the introduction of rodents on islands as an additional source of food for foxes. Thus, the Russians released ground squirrels on Kodiak and other islands, and later American fox trappers filled barrels with ground squirrels and "mice" and released them indiscriminately on islands to encourage newly imported fox populations.

Besides preying on the eggs and chicks of birds that nest on the surface of the ground or in burrows, ground squirrels, voles and other rodents, as well as rabbits destroy vegetation. On some islands with huge numbers of rodents, vegetation has been so extensively overgrazed that severe erosion is occurring. Rats have reached 82 percent of the world's islands via ships. Twenty-three islands between Kodiak and Attu have rats, and they also occur on some islands in the Alexander Archipelago as well as in certain coastal towns as far north as Nome. Rats reach islands uninhabited by humans mainly by shipwrecks. Most were introduced in the Aleutians during World

War II, but the danger is omnipresent that they will reach additional islands from grounded vessels. Unlike foxes, once rats become established on all but tiny islands they cannot be removed even with the liberal use of poisons. Unlike some countries like New Zealand that have active rat eradication programs, the U. S. Fish and Wildlife Service has not yet completed contingency plans to deal with maritime accidents in Alaska that could result in the infestation of more Alaska islands with rats and consequent devastation of nesting birds.

GAME ANIMALS

A whole host of animals have been introduced or relocated in Alaska for sport hunting or trapping, mainly on islands. In 1916 the Cordova Chamber of Commerce arranged the introduction of black-tailed deer from Southeast where they are native, to Hinchinbrook and Hawkins islands in Prince William Sound. Shortly thereafter deer were released on Kodiak, on islands in Yakutat Bay and on a few other islands. Other attempts to introduce deer, such as on the Homer Spit, failed.

Moose also were translocated to parts of Alaska where they did not occur naturally. They were released on Kalgin Island in Cook Inlet, in Berners Bay near Juneau and on the Copper River delta. Moose released on Kodiak Island and a few other locations did not survive.

Bison from Montana were introduced to several places on Alaska's mainland, starting in 1928 near Delta. They were also put on Popof Island in the Shumagins. Afognak Island near Kodiak and three islands in the Alexander Archipelago witnessed the introduction of elk, beginning in 1926. Mountain goats were released on Baranof Island in 1923 and about 30 years later on Chichagof, another nearby island in Southeast. Goats were established on Kodiak in the 1950s, also the island to which Dall sheep were translocated in the mid-1960s.

Caribou were transported to Adak Island in the central Aleutians by the Navy in 1958, and reindeer were released on St. Matthew, the Pribilofs, Hagemeister, Atka, Unalaska, Umnak and other islands. Since there were no wolves, bears or other natural predators, they quickly became too numerous for some islands to support, resulting in serious overgrazing and erosion. On St. Matthew Island, for example, the herd grew from 29 animals in 1944 to more than 6,000 in 1963, whereupon the population crashed to less than 50 following an extreme winter. Range damage currently is occurring on Hagemeister Island in Bristol Bay. Similarly, cattle were put on many islands, and on several they were later abandoned, necessitating removal to preclude further extensive damage to island vegetation and soils.

Other game mammals translocated to the Kodiak area or islands in Southeast included

In the 1950s, caribou were transported to some of the Aleutian Islands, to the Pribilofs and to Hagemeister Island in Bristol Bay. The islands lacked natural predators, and the caribou quickly overreached the islands' ability to support them. This led to severe degradation of the grazing range. (Roy M. Corral)

muskrat, beaver, hogs, marten, mink, raccoon, red squirrel, marmot and wolf. Pheasants, bobwhite quail and Chukar and Hungarian partridges were released at various dates and places, but only ring-necked pheasants survive in a few locations like the Kenai Peninsula. Spruce grouse and blue grouse were brought to Kodiak from other parts of the state, but none survived.

Of the numerous alien species released on hundreds of islands and in some mainland areas in Alaska, foxes by far have caused the most serious ecological consequences and still prove a major challenge to eradicate on certain islands. Reindeer, cattle and other ungulates also have considerably damaged several areas and no doubt compete with native species in certain situations. Introductions of alien animals also pose the threat of bringing diseases to native species. Altering the natural distribution and abundance of plants and animals that have evolved during great spans of time often brings dire consequences, especially to islands where ecosystems are more delicate because of less species diversity and where, often in the case of birds, unique nesting patterns developed in the absence of land predators.

Bats: Alaska's Flying Mammals

Huge snowflakes swirled thick around John Hastings and his dad, Ben, as they drove their skiff across Cholmondeley Sound. They were headed toward their hunting cabin on southwest Prince of Wales Island. Suddenly they glimpsed a cloak of black overhead. The undulating form seemed to be following them. John pulled out his binoculars for a better look. What he saw were bats.

"There were probably about 1,000 of them. I'd never seen as many," John said, recalling that November evening two years ago. The bats swarmed above them, flying along with the boat for about the next 15 minutes. The men watched the bats until they could see them no longer in the worsening snow squall and deepening dusk.

"It was kinda neat," recalls John. "We had to wonder what they wanted, what they were doing."

The Hastings are not the only ones. Alaska's bat buffs — and yes, there are a few — are fascinated by such encounters. So little is known about Alaska's bats that any story comes as welcome news, another piece in the puzzle of how these tiny, flying mammals survive in their northernmost range.

Little brown bats, Myotis lucifugus, *like this one are the most common of six bat species known to occur in Alaska, out of 42 species found in North America. A little brown bat can eat 600 mosquitoes an hour. (Merlin D. Tuttle, Bat Conservation International)*

Worldwide, there are lots of bats. More than 1,000 types of bats make up nearly a fourth of all mammal species on Earth. In places like the tropics, bats account for half the total types of mammals. Bats are highly developed, intelligent creatures, and they are the only mammals that fly. They feed at night, finding their way and prey by echolocation, a specialized form of sonar in which they bounce high-pitched signals off the surroundings. There are bats that feed only on fish, detecting fin ripples in the water and swooping down to gaff the fish with their barbed back feet. There are bats that eat fruit, bats that drink blood, carnivorous bats, and bats that feed only on frogs. They range in size from the world's smallest mammal — the Bumblebee bat of Thailand weighing in at less than a penny — to giant flying foxes with six-foot wingspans in Java.

Granted, the mere mention of bats brings on the shivers in some folks, and indeed the folklore of our culture casts bats as fearsome, disease-laden creatures. The Chinese, on the other hand, view bats as symbols of food, luck, prosperity and happiness and use images of bats in art and decoration. It is this attitude of which bats are most deserving, asserts Bat Conservation International, an Austin-based organization dedicated to global protection and conservation of these "gentle friends, essential allies."

Far from loathsome, bats instead are a vital link in the success of many different ecosystems. Most of the world's bats, about 70 percent, eat insects, helping control crop and disease-spreading pests. Of all the bats, less than one-third of a percent are blood-drinkers, all in Latin America, and less than half of a percent of those ever contract rabies. Yet, even vampire bats offer new discoveries to medicine in the anticoagulant they secrete. In West Africa, bats carry 90 to 98 percent of the "pioneer" seeds needed to begin forest regrowth on cleared lands. A recent Bat Conservation International study documented more than 300 plant species in the tropics alone that need bats for pollination or seed dispersal. More than 450 commercial products come from these plants, providing an important economy for developing countries.

Yet the status of bats is so poorly known that species are becoming extinct before they can be recognized as endangered. Nearly 40 percent of the bats in the United States are on the federal list of endangered species or candidates for it.

Alaska's bat profile likewise is little understood. Compared to other places, Alaska is bat poor. Only six species of bats have ever been found in Alaska, and they all are insect-eaters. Of those, the little brown bat, *Myotis lucifugus*, is most common. It ranges from Southcentral into the Interior and southwest to the Kodiak Island group. The others — the California bat, Keen's bat, the long-legged bat, the silver-haired bat and the big brown bat — have been found only once or twice in Alaska during the past century, and most of those occurrences have been in Southeast.

However, that may be changing. Alaska's bats are getting a closer look from a few scientists out to chart new bat ground. Alaska's bat researches are trying to find the rarer species, learn more about the little brown bats, and solve the big mystery of where Alaska's bats go in the winter.

Joe Cook is one of these researchers. As curator of mammals for the University of Alaska Museum in Fairbanks, he keeps records and specimens of all types of mammals in the state. While studies abound on bears, wolves and other big game, little work exists on small mammals like

A recent discovery of Keen's bats roosting among boulders near a hot springs on the Queen Charlotte Islands, British Columbia, encouraged Dr. Ed West to look for Keen's bats at a similar hot springs habitat on Chichagof Island in July 1992. Bats had been reported at the Chichagof location by Alaska Department of Fish and Game wildlife biologists Marilyn Sigman and Jeff Hughes. West and his assistant, biologist Una Swain, found a nursery colony of bats, but they were little browns rather than Keen's bats. West identified the bats from specimens he captured in a mist net. They spent three nights studying the colony with its newly emerging young. Eighty degree water flowed beneath the boulders, warming the roost that the bats reached through narrow openings between the boulders. Little brown bats normally roost in tree hollows and buildings, while Keen's bats often roost in trees and under bark. The discovery of bats roosting among boulders near hot springs is thought to be an unusual find. (Una Swain, courtesy of Dr. Ed West)

Dr. Ed West, a zoologist with the Alaska Natural Heritage Program, removes a little brown bat from a mist net on Chichagof Island. West has been looking for Keen's bats in southeastern Alaska, as part of a U.S. Forest Service project to identify rare species on its Alaska forest lands. (Una Swain, courtesy of Dr. Ed West)

shrews, voles and bats. Cook studied bats in the neotropics of South America and in the southwestern United States before coming to Fairbanks in 1990. He spent part of last summer in Kodiak looking at a colony of little brown bats.

"Although most of Alaska's bats are little brown guys, they may be doing some very, very interesting things that we just don't know about," he says. "Nobody has put much research time into looking at them."

Most of what is known about Alaska's bats concerns the habits and life cycle of the little browns, which are found throughout much of the northern United States and most of Canada. Little brown bats are just that — little and brown. They measure between three and four inches long with a eight-inch wingspread, and weigh only about 10 grams. These tiny mammals eat literally tons of insects, including mosquitoes. One little brown bat

can capture 600 mosquitoes an hour, an attribute that should endear this bat to most any Alaskan.

Jeff Hughes, a biologist with the Alaska Department of Fish and Game in Anchorage, keeps tabs on bats in Southcentral. Palmer, Wasilla and Big Lake, says Hughes, makes up the heart of Alaska's little brown bat country. He has seen bat colonies perhaps 1,000 members strong rise out of building eaves. He knows of sites in Southcentral where females congregate year after year, roosting by the hundreds in groups known as maternity colonies.

Male and female little browns mate in the fall, but the female holds the sperm in her uterus through winter. Come spring and Holy Conception Capers, Batman! The females in a maternity colony ovulate practically in unison and 20 days later, births begin bam, bam, bam, usually one baby to a bat. For a couple of weeks, the babies cling to their mothers. When the mothers fly out to feed, the babies stay in the cave and are tended by a few adults, maybe 1,000 baby bats in a clump. Within a month, the young are flying and feeding on their own.

Hughes hears each spring from people who are happy their bats are back. One woman, who lives off the Glenn Highway outside Palmer, calls at the first sign of bats returning to her garage. He also gets horrified calls from bat-phobics who want the creatures shooed from their homes and outbuildings. To them, he suggests

plugging the openings through which the bats come and go, either during the night while the bats are out feeding or after the first frost, by which time they most likely have taken leave for winter.

But where do Alaska's bats go in winter? No one knows, although researchers are batting around several theories. Perhaps they stay in the area, burrowing into cracks and crevices to hibernate. But bats are more likely to dry up than freeze. Bats' large wing membranes can desiccate quickly when cold temperatures zap moisture from the air. Perhaps Alaska's bats migrate to warmer, moister places to spend the winter, flying over the mountains into the maritime climate of coastal Southeast.

Dr. Ed West, a zoologist with the Alaska Natural Heritage Program in Anchorage, thinks that is a possibility. He has been stalking one of Alaska's rarer bats, *Myotis keenii* or Keen's long-eared bat. His interest in Keen's bat stems from work with the U.S. Forest Service in identifying rare species on forest service lands in Alaska. The forest service is required to maintain the biodiversity of its lands, and a step in doing that is determining what species may live there, documenting their occurrence and managing the land to maintain their habitat.

Keen's bat hangs out in coastal rain forests in a narrow band along the west coast from Washington to southeastern Alaska and neighboring British Columbia. At one time, Keen's bat was thought to belong to a larger population of bats covering the midwest to the east coast, but a study of bat skulls in the 1970s showed the two groups to be distinct. The eastern sister species roosts in trees, timber snags and under bark. The Forest Service hired West to find Keen's bat in its Alaska woods. The only time Keen's bat has been found here was in Wrangell in 1895. That is where West started his search last summer.

He stalked bats dusk to dawn, from 11 p.m. to about 3 a.m., setting his net in all sorts of batty-looking places in the city of Wrangell, around the island and along the lower Stikine River. Bat researchers use mist nets, with hair-thin meshing that can be strung over wide open areas, and square-framed Tuttle traps of monofilament lines, good for use in caves and across building openings. Because Alaska's bats look so similar when flying, identification depends on body measurements and fur coloring. West never netted a Keen's bat, but he did capture three long-legged bats. This species, *Myotis volans*, ranges from Atlin, British Columbia, through Alberta and south to central Mexico. It had been found in Alaska only once before, on Admiralty Island in 1907. West netted his long-legged bats at the top of a 30-foot-tall street light, where they were feeding on insects. West also found seven little brown bats that trip.

This summer, he is heading in a different direction on his second season of Keen's bat tracking. A recent discovery of Keen's bats roosting among boulders near a hot springs in the Queen Charlotte Islands, B.C., is sending West to similar habitats in Alaska.

But it is Prince of Wales Island in Southeast that may be Alaska's biggest bat retreat. The island is crisscrossed with a labyrinth of caves, hundreds of miles of underground tunnels and caverns that are just now beginning to be explored.

Jim Baichtal, a geologist with the U.S. Forest Service in Ketchikan, heads the cave management program that identifies significant cave resources of Tongass National Forest. An inventory began five years ago of these caves on Prince of Wales and nearby Dall Island, as part of the Federal Caves Resources Protection Act of 1988. Baichtal's fascination with Alaska's bats grew out of his caving work. Some of the caves contain mounds of droppings, and a few bat skulls, skeletons and hibernating live bats.

The discoveries are making quite a stir in Alaska's bat circles. What role do the caves play in bats' lives? "It's good potential the caves are really important," says West. "Obviously they have been used extensively at one time or another."

Keen's long-eared bat, Myotis keenii, frequents coastal rain forests along the west coast and has been found in Alaska only once, in Wrangell in 1895. This species has one of the smallest distribution ranges in North America. (Merlin D. Tuttle, Bat Conservation International)

The quantity of bat bones indicate historical use of at least some of the caves. Fresh evidence — droppings, wings and legs of insects, and a flesh-covered California bat skull, the most northern ever recorded — mean the caves are still being used. The last finding of California bats, *Myotis californicus*, in Alaska occurred in 1918, when two mummified specimens were found on Long Island in Southeast.

Baichtal's most recent discovery of hibernating bats may be one of the most exciting for Alaska's bat researchers. Maybe the caves, yet largely uncharted, are their winter homes.

In the meantime, Alaska's bat researchers are hoping to hear more and more about the state's flying mammals from people who see and find them around their homes.

"As we start to get out and talk to people, we're getting more reports," says West. "Bats are probably out there but because they're secret in behavior, people are just not aware of them."

SEEN ANY BATS LATELY?

Readers who want to report bat sightings can contact one of the following:

Joe Cook
University of Alaska Museum
907 Yukon Drive
Fairbanks, AK 99775-1200

Jim Baichtal
U.S. Forest Service,
Tongass National Forest
Federal Building
Ketchikan, AK 99901

Ed West
Alaska Natural Heritage Program
707 A Street, Suite 208
Anchorage, AK 99501

Jeff Hughes
Alaska Dept. of Fish and Game
333 Raspberry
Anchorage, AK 99518

The following information about your sighting is useful: Date and time; type of place; latitude and longitude, as nearly as possible; and estimated size of colony.

Avoid disturbing roosting bat colonies, handling live bats or killing them. People who find dead bats can freeze them in plastic bags and contact one of the men above to arrange for delivery. Since bats are nocturnal, activity during the day could mean the bat is sick and should be left alone. No cases of rabies carried by bats have ever been reported in Alaska, however.

OOPS...

Sharp-eyed reader Elliott Barske of Anchorage spotted an error in the Daylight Hours chart in Vol. 19, No. 2, *Alaska: The Great Land.*

To quote Mr. Barske, who works for the National Weather Service and keeps up on these matters, "[T]he times listed for Anchorage, and I assume the other cities, are based on the old time zones before they were changed to the current two time zone configuration. Also, daylight time is not figured in for the summer times. Thus the winter times (for Anchorage) are 1 hour too early, and the summer times are 2 hours too early." Mr. Barske kindly sent along the correct chart, shown at right.

SUMMER MAXIMUM:

	Sunrise	Sunset	Hours of Daylight
Barrow	*	*	24:00
Fairbanks	2:59 am	12:48 am	21:49
Anchorage	4:21 am	11:42 pm	19:21
Juneau	3:51 am	10:09 pm	18:18
Ketchikan	4:04 am	9:32 pm	17:28
Adak	6:27 am	11:10 pm	16:43

WINTER MINIMUM:

	Sunrise	Sunset	Hours of Daylight
Barrow	*	*	0:00
Fairbanks	10:59 am	2:41 pm	3:42
Anchorage	10:14 am	3:42 pm	5:28
Juneau	8:46 am	3:07 pm	6:21
Ketchikan	8:12 am	3:18 pm	7:05
Adak	9:52 am	5:38 pm	7:46

DON'T MISS YOUR
ALASKA GEOGRAPHIC.
NEWSLETTER INDEX!

This 10-page index contains an alphabetical listing of all subjects covered in the newsletters accompanying Volumes 15, Number 4, through Volume 18, Number 4. Also included is a complete list of all photographers whose work appears in those newsletters. To purchase this handy index, send $3.00 to:

ALASKA GEOGRAPHIC NEWSLETTER INDEX
P.O. Box 93370
Anchorage, AK 99509-3370

McKinley's Great Gorge Deeper Than Grand Canyon

What may be the deepest gorge in North America was measured successfully for the first time this summer by scientists from the Geophysical Institute, University of Alaska Fairbanks.

The Great Gorge, located on the south side of Mount McKinley, was found to be nearly 9,000 feet deep, making it deeper than the steepest valleys in the Grand Canyon and in Yosemite National Park. The measurement includes the ice of Ruth Glacier, which fills the bottom of the gorge, combined with the height of the vertical walls surrounding it.

Forty-mile-long Ruth Glacier drains the southern slopes of Mount McKinley as it flows through the granite-walled Great Gorge. Mountains such as Moose's Tooth, Mount Dickey, the Shield and Rooster Comb rise up along its sides. Most of Ruth Glacier is located within Denali National Park and Preserve.

Commissioned by Bradford Washburn, honorary director of the Boston Museum of Science and a former National Advisor for The Alaska Geographic Society, researchers set out to find the bottom of the gorge two years ago. First, they tried to determine the total depth of the Great Gorge by using conventional ice radar instruments to measure the thickness of Ruth Glacier. But that did not work because the ice in the gorge was too thick for standard instruments to penetrate.

In summer 1992, the scientists tried again. Led by Associate Professor Keith Echelmeyer of the Geophysical Institute and Institute graduate Ted Clarke, a crew returned to the gorge with seismic instruments, some of which triggered small explosions powerful enough to send seismic waves through Ruth Glacier to the bottom of the gorge.

Through this process, the scientists were able to determine the depth and the shape of the gorge and the glacier. The 9,000-foot-deep gorge is U-shaped and less than a mile wide at the top, and the ice contained within it is more than 3,800 feet thick.

Echelmeyer also measured how fast the glacier moved through the Great Gorge using a satellite-based surveying method. He found the ice moved an average speed of 3.3 feet per day, which is relatively fast for a glacier.

Washburn, who has mapped both Mount McKinley and Mount Everett, said he has been waiting for 55 years to find out the depth of the Great Gorge. He suspected it would be among the deepest gorges in the world.

"Every flake of snow that falls on the southeastern flanks of Mount McKinley pours downward and is squeezed through that milewide gorge," Washburn said.

—University of Alaska Fairbanks

Forgotten War Remembered 50 Years Later

Aleutian veterans and Aleut refugees are remembered at a ceremony at Unalaska commemorating the 50th anniversary of the bombing of Dutch Harbor by the Japanese in June 1942.

**STORY AND PHOTOS
BY CARY ANDERSON**

A half century ago, a fleet of Japanese warplanes terrorized the military post at Unalaska, strafing the town with machine guns and pounding defense facilities with a string of bombs. Columns of smoke rose from the fiery explosions as servicemen scrambled to defend the Aleutian port at Dutch Harbor. The air strike marked the beginning of a bloody World War II campaign that would spread to other Aleutian Islands including Kiska and Attu, as Japan fought to claim the Territory of Alaska as its own. Casualty estimates vary, but by some accounts as many as 76 Americans were killed and about 50 were wounded in the two-day attack.

On June 3, 1992, a pair of camouflage C-130 aircraft touched down at Unalaska carrying close to 100 survivors of the Dutch Harbor assault. The special field trip to honor these veterans, now in their 70s and 80s, was arranged by the Alaska National Guard. Most of the former soldiers were members of an Arkansas National Guard unit that was assigned to protect Alaska at the onset of the war.

The returning vets were treated like long absent local heroes in the community of Unalaska. Lodging and meals were free. There was no charge for the shuttle buses, taxis and family cars that were used for personal tours of whatever area landmarks the vets wanted to visit. Everyone in town seemed eager to help.

Morris Agrice, 73, a former Army anti-aircraft gunner from Texas, hitched a ride up a steep, winding and muddy backroad to the summit of Ballyhoo Hill, where he stepped outside the car for a look around. Braced against a biting wind with nearly horizontal rain, Agrice recalled even worse weather when he was stationed on the hill. "It was unbelievable. The wind was blowing the snow and sleet. We looked like ice balls with ice hanging all over our mouths

Morris Agrice, a former anti-aircraft gunner stationed at Unalaska, inspects an old bunker where he stood watch during World War II.

and eyes." Agrice then crouched near the canopy of an old bunker and peered inside. Graffiti was scrawled on the interior walls, and broken bottles littered the floor. But the structure was still intact, and so were the memories of the many days and nights he had spent there watching for enemy planes.

Another Aleutian war veteran, Les Lesko, 75, said the constant threat of attack and the severe storms were nothing compared to

the homesickness he suffered.

The former Navy munitions supplier's voice began to crack as he described having to leave his girlfriend in Clarksville, La. Fifty year later, his heart was breaking again with the vividness of the memory. "We were deeply in love," he gasped, tears streaming from behind his dark sunglasses. "I thought, Dear God, let me get back and see her." Lesko said his feelings about attending the reunion were mixed. "It's

Former Navy munitions supplier Les Lesko examines the replica of a Japanese Zero fighter plane in the hangar at Unalaska.

something you want to leave behind, but now that I'm here, I feel much better."

Not all of the recollections were somber. And the good-natured camaraderie of the vets was frequently apparent. One gentleman sharing a beer with some old war buddies was boasting of his superior skill in firing a 50mm machine gun. One of his friends interrupted and shouted, "Hey, the only thing you did was shoot the sky full of holes so the Japanese could get through." Everyone within earshot roared with laughter.

Commemorative activities capping the reunion included the flyby of a replica Japanese Zero fighter plane and a memorial

ceremony. The ceremony honored the veterans of Dutch Harbor and recognized the Aleuts who were evacuated from their homes to internment camps in southeastern Alaska. Many Aleuts never returned to their ancestral island homes. An estimated 10 percent of them died in government refugee camps from poor living conditions and inadequate health care.

Lt. Col. John Bishop, addressing the crowd near the end of the ceremony, said, "Through the works of historians together with the members of the press, the nation is learning again about the sacrifices that all of the veterans made, and the Aleut evacuees, during the forgotten war of the Aleutian campaign."

Pack Creek Popularity Brings Rules

One of Southeast's premier bear-watching areas has become so popular that the U.S. Forest Service and the Alaska Department of Fish and Game have instituted regulations on the number of visitors. The regulations are designed to enhance a visitor's experience and to prevent any mishaps with the bears. Pack Creek, near Windfall Harbor off Seymour Canal on Admiralty Island's eastern shore, has long seen a congregation of brown bears during seasonal salmon runs. The area was also for decades the home of Stan Price, the bear man of Admiralty. For years, Price, the bears and occasional visitors got along just fine. But the increase in tourism in Southeast and the concomitant interest in wilderness tourism has pushed the number of visitors at Pack Creek to 1,100 during the peak season in 1991. These increases raised concern about the possibility of an unpleasant bear-human incident.

To head off any of these encounters, U.S. Forest Service and Alaska Department of Fish and Game staff worked out a permit system to control the number of human visitors. Beginning in 1992, from June 1 to September 10 visitors are limited to 24 a day. Permits are not required for visits to Pack Creek outside the June-September period. Reservations for the permits can be made in advance, although officials are setting aside four permits per day for reservations made within three days. For reservations contact: Admiralty Island National Monument, 8461 Old Dairy Road, Juneau, Alaska 99801, (907) 586 8790; or U.S. Forest Service Visitors Center, 101 Egan Drive, Juneau, Alaska 99801.

Alaska's Pintail Population Stable

While their numbers have decreased precipitously in the rest of the United States and Canada, the number of northern pintail ducks in Alaska has remained stable during the past 36 years, according to Bill Eldridge, migratory bird biologist with the U. S. Fish and Wildlife Service.

In spring 1992, just under half of all pintails counted in the United States and Canada were in Alaska. According to Eldridge, these numbers often reflect habitat conditions elsewhere. "Throughout the 1980s, a series of drought years decreased waterfowl breeding habitat in the Canadian prairies to a level that has not recovered, and the continental pintail population declined. When drought reduces habitat, some pintails overfly their normal breeding areas, coming to Alaska and northern Canada where the water supply is more stable. Fortunately, good snow cover and rainfall improved conditions in the prairies this year."

Better conditions on the prairies led to an overall increase of pintails on the continent and a corresponding decrease in Alaska. Although the 1992 continental pintail population level lies 54 percent below a 36-year average, pintail numbers increased 16 percent from 1991 with improved breeding conditions in the southern prairies to 2,098,100 birds. Alaska's pintail population dropped 19 percent from 1991 to 900,000 birds, possibly because more birds remained on the improved breeding areas in the prairies this year. These figures are based on a May and June 1992 breeding pair survey of pintails and other ducks in Alaska, Canada, the Dakotas and Montana.

True heralds of the seasons, pintails are among the earliest migrants to arrive in Alaska in the spring, and they are the earliest ducks to leave the state in the fall. By mid-August to early September, most pintails are on their way to wintering areas along the California coast and in Mexico. (U.S. Fish and Wildlife Service)

SHARING

I was recently loaned the quarterly issue of Alaska Geographic on Skagway, and found it extremely interesting for several reasons.

First of all, my first husband (deceased in 1975) grew up in Skagway and through visits after our marriage I became familiar with the town and with many of the people mentioned....

Then, unexpectedly, I found my husband's picture as a youth in the group of basketball players on page 63; he was Lewis Dahl, and I must correct your description of him. He did, indeed, become a doctor, receiving his M.D. from the University of Pennsylvania with subsequent training in internal medicine at Massachusetts General Hospital in Boston. But contrary to your description of him, he never went to Johns Hopkins. He worked at the Rockefeller Institute for Medical Research (now Rockefeller University) following his Boston training, then worked in medical research at Brookhaven National Laboratory in Upton, Long Island, N.Y. from 1952 until his death in 1975.

Secondly, ... Lewis Dahl's father, Dr. Peter I. Dahl, was the only doctor in Skagway from 1925-1950. He was an important, respected and much loved man. For 25 years he delivered all the babies, cared for the sick and injured and certainly saved many lives. When he retired in 1950 the whole town feted him and subsequently named a new Skagway medical center in his honor — Dahl Memorial Hospital — which I visited in 1977.

—Marilyn Dahl Krumhansl
Amherst, Massachusetts

ALASKA GEOGRAPHIC® BACK ISSUES

From time to time readers write in to inquire about obtaining copies of out-of-print back issues of *ALASKA GEOGRAPHIC*®. Archie H. Stevens has advised us that he has copies of back issues from the mid-1970s. Interested readers may contact Mr. Stevens at 2196 AuSable Point Road, East Tawas, MI 48730.

PLEASE DO NOT FEED THE SEA LIONS

LEFT: *A sea lion swims through St. Paul Harbor with an arrow in its back in this 1989 photo. (Chlaus Lotscher)*

RIGHT: *A crewman feeds a Steller sea lion in St. Paul Harbor on Kodiak in this 1983 photo. This species is now on the threatened list and may be put on the endangered list under the Endangered Species Act because of drastic declines in their population in western Gulf of Alaska and Aleutian waters. Marmot Island near Kodiak once had one of the world's largest Steller sea lion rookeries, but the population decline has allowed Forrester Island's colony in Southeast to surpass that of Marmot. (Jim Simmen)*

Kodiak's boat harbor is a popular place with sea lions and people who want to see these jumbo members of the seal family. But a word of caution: feeding sea lions is illegal. And dangerous. "These are very big animals with a mouthful of teeth," says Ken Hansen, a special agent with the National Marine Fisheries Service in Kodiak.

The number of sea lions hanging out in Kodiak's harbor has increased in recent years, and so have the problems associated with them. Hansen estimates 40 to 50 sea lions frequent downtown Kodiak's waterfront. "It's a great place to see them. Just hang out at the harbor and one will wander by eventually. They're quite the tourist draw but they do have potential for problems."

They haul out on docks, basically blocking other users until they decide to jump back in the water. They climb aboard fishing boats, where they eat scrap fish from nets and decks. Brazen sea lions have even chased away customers on one commercial fuel dock, where they like to congregate. The dock is adjacent to a cannery dock where the animals have found food in the past. The increase in sea lions in the harbor seems to be related to the growth of boats fishing for pollock and cod since the mid-1980s. These groundfish are caught year-round, which translates to a continual supply of food in harbor waters as fishing crews sort their catch and hose down nets and decks.

What bothers federal and city officials is that people have deliberately fed sea lions to get them out of the water for pictures or whatever. And the animals have been harrassed; rocks have been thrown at them and one was even shot with an arrow. Stopping these abuses has become an ongoing campaign of public education and media attention.

People caught feeding, harassing, hunting, capturing and killing sea lions can be prosecuted under the federal Marine Mammal Protection Act. Feeding, as defined by federal law, does not include the routine discard of bycatch during fishing or the routine discharge of wastes or fish byproducts from fish processing plants. The City of Kodiak also prohibits deliberately feeding sea lions, with a fine of $300. Harbor master Corky McCorkle said a dozen warnings have been issued, but so far no fines. "Overall, things are getting better," says Hansen. "It's a matter of people being aware."

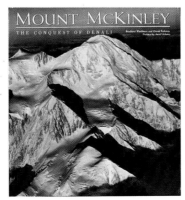
Mount McKinley: The Conquest of Denali, by Bradford Washburn and David Roberts, preface by Ansel Adams; Harry N. Abrams, Inc., New York; 206 pages, 118 black-and-white and color photos, eight maps, bibliography and index, hardcover with dust jacket, $60.

Editor's note: *Brad Washburn's and David Roberts' new book on Mount McKinley is sure to be a classic, and we asked Bob Henning, president emeritus of The Alaska Geographic Society, to comment on the book and his long-time friendship with Dr. Washburn.*

Certainly every student of Alaska's great mountain must have this superb volume in their library, but so should anyone who just collects Alaskana. This is a book that belongs with Bancroft [Hubert Howe Bancroft's *History of Alaska 1730-1885*], Rex Beach's *The Spoilers*, Robert Service and the rest of the great titles that speak to the wonders of the North, the beauty, the rich promises, the ever-present challenge of adventure, but most of all because this book is really a private look into one man's passionate affair with a mountain.

I traveled with Brad Washburn and his wife, Barbara, (the first woman to climb Denali) in Switzerland when a group of us from Alaska went over to see how the Swiss managed their mountains. Everywhere we went we saw peaks that Washburn and his wife had climbed and heard from veteran Swiss mountain climbers about when the Washburns experienced the exciting Matterhorn, Jungfrau and the rest. But I keep remembering their honeymoon when the Washburns climbed Mount Crillon in Glacier Bay National Park, and I remember a $25,000 Fairchild camera that I believe was built for Brad's Mount McKinley (Denali now) expeditions and the beginnings of his aerial mapping of the Denali family of peaks.

We talked often of Denali, and you could always feel the love of this man for that mountain. And you'll read it in his words and in his great photos.

The University of Alaska is richer for Washburn's gift of a great plaster bas relief of Denali, and a priceless collection of maps and photos and research.

Thank you, both of you wonderful mountain-obsessed Washburns, for your gifts and for sharing with us an Alaska love for the same mountain.

Published by
THE ALASKA GEOGRAPHIC SOCIETY

Penny Rennick,
EDITOR

Kathy Doogan,
PRODUCTION DIRECTOR

L.J. Campbell,
STAFF WRITER

Jan Westfall,
MARKETING MANAGER

Kevin Kerns,
CIRCULATION/DATABASE MANAGER

© 1992 by The Alaska Geographic Society